An Amateurs guide to: Killing it

Shannon Dennis

Acknowledgements:

I want to dedicate this book to everybody that has ever supported me. You know who you are, and I truly couldn't have done it without you. Thank you for your ongoing and consistent inspiration. Never have I gone a day without a smile, and for that, I thank you, every single one of you.

An Amateurs Guide to: Killing It

Chapters

An Amateurs guide to: Killing It

Shannon Dennis

An Amateurs Guide to: Killing It

Introduction

Okay, here it goes. Never would I have thought that I would be an author. Never would I have thought that I would be somebody offering advice to anybody else. However, the truth is, there is never a specific time that it is "right" for you to write a book. I am continually learning, constantly growing, so how can I write a book on how to better yourself, if I am not an expert in life? However, you know what, if you can read this book and pick up even one thing that makes you realise what life has to offer you, and that there are no boundaries, then all this was worth it. The hours I have put into writing this, every single moment, worth it, to allow you to understand that you are never alone in this journey and there is always somebody there to help you. You are killing it, even before reading this, you are killing it at life, for the fact that you're still here. That proves something, you might be having the best day of your life or the worst, but the fact you have even picked up this book and are considering reading it, is you telling yourself that it is time for a change in your life, and for you to bring me along on that journey is a real honour.

I'm not perfect. Nobody is perfect. Let me tell you a little story. I was once writing a blog about dealing with stress and stopped writing it for I was mid-way through having a mini-meltdown because I felt overwhelmed. I've been writing blogs on how to not be a hypocrite, but I felt like a hypocrite because I was telling people how to deal with overwhelm and stress even though I was experiencing these emotions, but that's what made me realise that it is okay to feel that way. The moment you understand you are in control of your feelings and that your thoughts cause your emotions is the moment you start to deal with problems instead of letting them consume you. This book is not me being the 'perfect human' and showing you how to live the perfect life. However, this book aims to show you that it is okay to feel the way you do. I want to introduce to you the importance of self-love and offer you advice on how to deal with your emotions. You can do it. You are strong enough. I believe in you. The very fact you have made it to the end of reading this introduction proves that you are ready to commit to bettering yourself. For that, I couldn't be prouder of you.

As I was re-reading this from start to finish, I think it is pretty obvious to see how the tone changes. This book is a natural progression of my mindfulness. I was talking to my friend after reading it through, and I was saying how I was thinking about re-writing some of the chapters or moving them around, and her response hit the nail on the head. She said, "Shannon, this shows your natural progression, and that's the realist thing you can give to your audience." She was right. This book represents advice from my perspective on my journey; every single one of these chapters was written in the moment of feeling like it was relevant to my life. So every word that I write, I've experienced, this book is real emotion and built on experience. I never set out for this book to be a fake facade on how you could improve your life because I'm still working on mine. However, I advise you to read the chapters that you feel are relevant to you at that particular time, who says a book needs to be read from start to finish? So mainstream. Use this book as you need to because after all, I'm no life professional, I'm an amateur, but I am killing it, and you can too once you've unlocked the willpower to do so.

An Amateurs Guide to: Killing It

An Amateurs Guide to: Killing it

Shannon Dennis

Chapter 1: Coping with Heart Break

Having your heart broken sucks. At that time, nothing is worse, right? Your whole world falls apart, and you feel lost. Consumed by your own company and eaten by your own emotion. It is shit. You miss them. Find yourself alone a lot of the time. You forget who you were once before. You've forgotten how to love yourself. People deal with heartbreak differently, and that's okay. If you want to jump straight into something else, then that's okay. However, what happens to a lot of us is we "fall" for someone else, involve yourself in blissful avoidance, where everything seems fine. When in fact, you're trying to build a house on cracked foundations, and you haven't given yourself the time to get over the hurt that came with that heartbreak.

It's difficult when you tell yourself that you have moved on. Every single time you see that person, your heart starts racing, your hands turn sweaty, and you instantly feel like you're going to vomit. Here's the shit thing about heartbreak. That feeling will never "just" disappear; it takes an abundance of self-love to move from that place that you fall into. You end up kidding yourself that you are okay when in real fact, we both know you're not. This brings me onto my first rule of dealing with heartbreak, understanding that it's okay to hurt.

Social media stalking WILL NOT HELP YOU. You're most likely going to run into things that you do not want to see. However, you become obsessed with checking their every update. Every 'like' they make on Instagram, you become a member of the CSI, searching for any information you can get on them. If you want to deal with heartbreak, immersing yourself in everything they do is not going to help you. I know one of the hardest parts of heartbreak is unfollowing them, and it's a big step to go from knowing everything about them to no longer have any tabs on their life. The time that you decide to take the 'no stalking step' is entirely up to you. This whole journey is entirely up to you, the most important message to take away from this entire thing, is

your process of overcoming this, doesn't have a time

scale. You have all the time in the world, to decide when

the time is right for you. Other people's opinions on you

'moving on' are irrelevant, this is about you. Everything

about this journey is going to be difficult. I'm not going

to lie to you, but it's not impossible. You're stronger than

you think. You might think that's it's childish to unfriend

them, or what if they judge you, but you need to put

yourself first at this time. Burning cyber bridges will help

you in the long run. I promise you.

If it takes you crying every single night until you

physically cannot cry another tear, then so be it. If it

means you scream your head off with anger in a field

where nobody is around, then so be it. At the end of the

day, you're the only one who will genuinely know within yourself when you're over it. It may take a week, it may take a decade, but there is no rush. Time is on your side. Being emotional is not a weakness; crying is not a sign of failure. Once all those raw emotions are out of your system, only then can you think about rebuilding yourself. So, I'm telling you now if you want to cry for 6 hours, go for it. I'm not going to stand here and tell you 100 reasons how to stop yourself being sad about heartbreak and how to get over it because I honestly believe it's a personal thing. So you can go looking for advice from Cosmopolitan™ and Buzzfeed™ articles, but only you will know when that time comes, and when it does, you will be unstoppable.

The next step in heartbreak is learning to know yourself. Okay, let's say, you've cried yourself to sleep for the past fortnight, or year, or however long it may be, and you're finally at the stage where you think you are ready to move on. You need to love yourself first before you even attempt to love somebody else. You need to find yourself, learn your personality, and understand who you are as an independent individual. I'm not saying you need to introduce yourself in the mirror, or where a name badge to make you feel like you're a new person. However, the hardest part of heartbreak is regaining the independence that you once had, that independence you never realised you lost. Admitting the fact that you need to learn to know yourself again, is the first step in understanding yourself. The best thing you can do here is to write down a list of everything you want to achieve. Make a one -

year plan, a five - year plan, and a ten - year plan. Write everything down, from your feelings to what you are grateful for. Write this plan as if you are in that moment where you want to be. This will give you incentives and goals to work towards and will make you feel like a boss who definitely has their shit together (we'll go into this in more detail later on).

Now, it's time for you to redistribute your time and work back from those goals that you have now set yourself. Let's be honest; you now have a lot more time on your hands; your schedule may even be completely free. Because you are through the emotional stage of heartbreak, you can now work on focusing your time on becoming the person you want to be, the person you will be. To clarify, we're not doing this for them; we're not doing this as a "fuck you to your ex." We're doing this for you; you are the driver in your car. If the "fuck you" should arise, ride it, but this should never be out of spite, this is for your life.

So, now, you are truly in charge of your time, you do not need to take into consideration your partners feelings if you go out with that specific friend that they may not like anymore or the fact you want to go for a work dinner on their birthday, because they are no longer there. So, what do you do now? You take up every single lost opportunity that you may have left behind because you put them first. You reconnect with people you may have blocked out of your life. You go for dinner with that friend you haven't seen in months because you haven't had time. You take the time now to stay late at work to make sure that everything is done, not for anybody else, but for yourself. If you want to start bell ringing as a hobby, do it, you want to take an art class? Do it. Nobody is stopping you; you are you, your independency will hit you back in full force. You can fear it and hide inside, or you can take it and live in every single moment and do everything that you want to do. Last year, I went on five holidays, you know why? Because I wanted to, I'm not rich, by any means, but travelling is something I have always wanted to do, "there is no time like the present." Fuck it.

Admitting to yourself that the relationship is over, is one of the most essential parts. Reading through old text messages, old voicemails, wearing their clothes, is not going to help you. Looking for a reason to blame yourself, is not going to help you. Also, assuming things are your fault will not help you. When your ex-boyfriend or ex-girlfriend tells you the reason that they are ending the relationship, listen to that. Do not fight the reason in your head and convince yourself that there is a glance of hope that you will get back together, and everything will be okay again. If you end up getting back with them and that's what truly makes you happy, then amazing. I couldn't be happier for you. However, dealing with heartbreak is fixing yourself, and a part of that is not putting yourself in denial. The brain reacts to heartbreak the same way as it does to someone who is withdrawing themselves from Class A drugs, and therefore, you need to understand that with removing a relationship, comes side effects.

"It's not you; it's me." Instead of feeling out of control, reassure yourself that they have commitment issues. Don't waste your time and energy, begging for a reason. Accept that it's over. Do not spend time in denial. Put yourself first and focus your energy on self-love and working on yourself. The earlier you work on mending yourself, the easier your grieving will be because you're accepting the hurt. The first step in dealing with heartbreak is admitting that your heart is broken.

The first thing that people do when they have their heartbroken is they turn bitter. It's easily done. You feel the anger take over your whole body, and you will do anything to get "back at them." Right? Sending them bitter messages to make yourself feel better. When in fact, that's not helping anybody is it? You feel better for the 2 minutes after you've sent it, you feel empowered, in control but then, let's be honest, 20 minutes later you feel just as shit as you did before you sent it. The empowerment has gone, the moment has passed, and now you're back to square one.

When someone says to you, be the bigger person, as cliché as it sounds, taking the higher ground will give you more empowerment than any message you can send. Trust me, I know it's hard not to turn bitter, we've all been there, but being the better person and staying kind-hearted, is always the better option. Stay true to yourself; you're more than sinking to the level of throwing shots below the belt. You owe yourself more than that as an individual. There is nothing better than the feeling of knowing that you still have self-respect, even with a

23

broken heart. Stay classy and own it. So, I'm giving you the opportunity here to do the best thing for you. "Moving on" is a scary concept and at times you will think it's impossible, but I'm telling you, you'll get there. One step at a time. The staircase looks terrifying when you're at the bottom of it, seems a lot higher than it is. All you need to do is look at the first step. One step at a time will get you there. There's no rush; you have nothing but time, It's okay.

You might be thinking; it's easier said than done. I, for one, completely understand that. I've been there, been in a relationship for five years, and thought to myself at times that I would never be okay again. Felt that he was the only one for me, and without him, I would never be happy again. However, I'm telling you from personal experience, the moment you realise that you control your own emotions is the moment you start to coach yourself into "getting over it". When I say "getting over someone" I don't mean you forget about them. I'm not saying ignore the memories. I'm not suggesting you go home and throw away every photo you ever have of them. Still, hold the memories, but what I am saying is do not allow yourself to think the only reason that you were ever happy was because of them. You still had good days; you still smiled when they weren't around. Your friends and family are going to be your most significant anchor at this time. They will be there for you, try not to shut yourself away. If you want to lock yourself in your room and eat a whole tub of Ben and Jerry's and listen to Lewis Capaldi's entire album, do it. However, do it with a friend. You do not have to deal with your emotions alone. I'm telling you, talking to someone is the best feeling.

 I've struggled for a while with feeling like I'm burdening friends with my problems. You may also feel this. However, one thing I learned (albeit the hard way) is it's okay to talk to people about your problems. It's okay to let go and rant to them for hours on the phone about how upset you are because your ex has liked another girl/boy's photo on Instagram. I understand. And it's okay. If that helps with your process of moving on, allow your emotions to happen. Observe them and let them pass through. Try not to waste energy by focussing on the negatives and what you have lost. Use the emotion you have and channel it to doing something productive. Write blogs, make songs, write a book, pick up a new hobby, do something that you have never done before. You will not be the only person in the world struggling with heartbreak. Make your content relatable, and you'll be away. Not only will you gain a support network for yourself, but you will also be getting your name "out there." People will start to follow your brand, your person for making content that relates to them. DREAM BIG. You could turn yourself into an internet sensation with your content overnight if you put your mind to it. Also, there's no better message to send someone who broke your heart than success.

People have always said to me that I'm so erratic, and I will hold my hands up and agree that there is no method to this madness. I pick up new hobbies, ALL THE TIME. However, what many people don't know is that these hobbies have mainly stemmed from when my heart has been hurting, and I needed a distraction. However, I've then turned the distraction into a way of channelling emotion, and I can only encourage you to do this. To find new things, because honestly, learning a new skill, is so rewarding, it pushes you to new boundaries and shows you what you are truly capable of.

The most important part of dealing with heartbreak is not letting it define you. Going from using pronouns such as "we" to using pronouns like "I" is tough. Gaining your independence back is tough. It's okay. That is okay. However, it's also okay to remember the memories you had together when you were "we." It's okay to go to the places that you went together. That will take time, but a pronoun is not going to define who you are. To move on, you need to reconnect with who you were before the relationship. You need to find yourself again, and the only way you're going to be able to do that is through giving yourself the time you deserve and getting to know and appreciate yourself again. You will love again, but you need to love yourself first.

This chapter aimed to try and explain that it is okay to be sad; it's okay to be angry; it's okay to be non-affected by heartbreak. Emotions will change, one moment you'll be absolutely fine and the next minute you find yourself welling up at the smell of a specific clothes store because that's where your ex used to shop. It's okay. It's okay to be emotional. However, heartbreak does not define who you are. You're still here, reading this, so you've taken the first step in trying to help yourself, you're reading advice, all be it from a twenty-one-year-old who is experiencing the same things as you are right now and is trying to collate emotion in the form of a book to help other people, but hey, advice is advice, right? So, if you've gotten to the end of this chapter and you think "well, I've read that, and I'm still not over them." Good. I'm glad you haven't read this, and you are magically cured of your heartbreak because that won't happen. However, there will be little keys of information in this chapter that might help you understand your worth as a human being and how truly amazing you are. It will be okay, you are still here, no matter how dark it seems now. I promise you, however cliché it sounds, things will get better.

An Amateurs Guide to: Killing It

Chapter Two: Dealing With your Ex

There are two types of ex. You've probably got ex's that you saw for two weeks and they cut you off for "no reason," and you've got the ex's that have genuinely destroyed you, right? Tore your heart right from your chest, made you cry a thousand tears, feel lower than you ever have before? The term "long term relationship" is bullshit. People instantly judge you on how "heartbroken" you are over somebody based on the time you spent together. "Oh, you've only been together a couple of months, why are you still crying over it." See, time is irrelevant. The connection is so important. Your feelings towards that person are the reason why you react the way you do. So, by somebody else judging you for the length of time you've spent with them is bullshit. The memories that you two shared; the laughter you shared; that is what is relevant, and I guess that it was makes it so hard to deal with your ex. Going from the feeling of being someone's "one and only" to being just a stranger on the street, is pretty hard going. Going from a "We" to an "I" is something that isn't easy to get your head around. Learning to be your own person again and trying your best to cope with seeing them as their own being as well as yourself as an individual rather than being a couple, isn't fun, it isn't easy, and it takes some getting used to.

You might be reading this and thinking that it's not even relevant to you. Hey, you might not have ever even had a boyfriend or girlfriend yet, and that's cool. However, I bet you've been talking to people before, and they've suddenly cut you off for random reasons, right? Below are some of the reasons that people will most probably give you to cut things off for a while and what they mean.

Excuse number one: "I just want to be friends."

How many times have you had that said to you? Then contemplated the whole relationship "thing" and deemed yourself as un-loveable forever and you're going to die alone with seven cats, right? Okay, hold on hun. When somebody tells you they want to be friends, what this usually means is they love you for who you are, but they would like the freedom of the single life. They are not ready to cut you out of their life altogether; you bring a vibe to their day that makes them feel good. However, they're looking to still have the freedom of not having a relationship. They want to be able to "do what they want" whether that be travel or go out every night; everyone has their reasons. However, mainly, the reason people want to be friends is that they see you like more of a support network rather than a romantic partner. Don't be thinking that this is the end of the world, being friends can be hard, especially when the feelings were there before, and it's difficult to "turn them off." If you find that the case and you do not believe you can fully be friends with them if you cannot be romantically involved with them, then let me introduce you to the "No contact rule."

The No Contact Rule

This will be referred to a lot during this chapter, so take note and fully understand what this rule means. It does exactly what it says on the tin. NO CONTACT. Do not message them, do not stalk their Instagram feed for 4 hours every day, do not ring them, do not Facebook message them. Do not turn up at their house with 600 roses and beg for them back. You're better than that (we both know that). The no contact rule is aimed to be a bitchy move. It's to help you either move forward. The no contact rule is difficult, however totally worth it in the long run. No pain, No Gain. NOTE: The no contact rule doesn't have to be permanent. It can be, however long you need it to be to allow yourself to come to terms with the breakup.

So, we all know that feelings are not like a light switch, no matter how much you want them to be, they don't work like that (unfortunately). So, how do you deal with someone just wanting to be friends with you? Use the non-contact rule to ground yourself, allow yourself to re-adjust back to how you were before without them (we'll discuss strategies for this later, don't panic). Give it some time. When you are ready, drop them the odd message asking them how they're doing, or a FaceTime catch up. I'm not talking about going all in and messaging every day all day, just the odd chat to let them know you're still there and that you are ready to be friends again.

There is no telling how long this time is. It may be a week, it may be a year, but that's okay, do not feel like you should be "over it by now" because only you truly know how you feel and when you're ready to bring them back into your life, then go for it. However, until then, take your time and do not rush it.

The thing is here, "I just want to be friends" and "I'm not ready for a relationship at the moment" are easily confused, even by the person who is giving you the excuse. However, we'll discuss that next. So, the notes to take from "I just want to be friends" is give yourself the time to get your head around the fact that there will not be romantic involvement, but you both obviously got on well together, therefore take the time away from them until you're ready, then bridge the friendship back. If you never feel that you are fully prepared to become friends again, then that is also okay. You do you, and that is fine, it's not an easy thing to do. Keep yourself as a priority.

Excuse number 2: "I'm just not ready for a relationship at the moment."

I wouldn't personally class this one as an excuse to stop talking to you. This is more of a request for space. When people say they're not ready for a relationship now, they are usually carrying much emotional baggage that they feel they need to sort through first. With this, try your hardest not to become bitchy, instead focus your energy on being there for them and being understanding. We all have our issues that we chose not to share with people, even the people closest to us. It becomes so easy to push people away and isolate yourself. This "excuse" can be linked quite closely with "I'm not sure what I want right now." Try not to hate your ex if they tell you that they're not ready for a relationship; there might be 101 reasons of why they can't, they might feel like they do not want to drag you through their problems. The best thing you can do in this situation is to be supportive and understanding. That can be difficult, I know, especially if you have invested a lot of time into that person, we all understand that it can be frustrating. However, getting angry at the situation will not fix it, if anything, you will cause the person to isolate themselves more. I'm not saying stay emotionally invested, but a message now and again will not hurt anybody, and if anything, make your ex realise that you still care about them and they are not alone.

Excuse number 3: "I'm not sure what I want right now.'

This is a tricky one because the only thing here that you can do is try and accept the fact that you must give them time and space. It might just not be a good time; let them decide. However, don't think that my advice is for you to wait like a sitting duck for them to come back potentially. No, use the time to work on yourself. I don't mean work out how to be that person's ideal girlfriend or boyfriend, I mean work on a project you've been waiting to do but haven't had the time, or start a new hobby, learn a new language. Find something to occupy your mind, work on your personal development. In this time, work out whether this relationship is what you want in your mind and if you're willing to sacrifice the uncertainty at that moment in time for that person. Always put yourself first.

Excuse number four: "I've met someone else."

This is probably one of the worse excuses you can hear if you do not know how to deal with it. However, guess what, lucky for you, you're still here reading, so let's work through this. So, I'm not going to make any decisions for you, but to know your self-worth is the most important thing here. If cheating was involved in this, you seriously need to consider whether you want to go back there. If you do, then there is nobody stopping you. Fuck everybody else's opinion, fuck what your friends say, this is about your happiness, and if they genuinely care about you, they will understand and respect your decision, whatever it may be. However, you need to remember that you are worth so much more than feeling like you're not enough. You are better than that. With this one, I know I've said it a thousand times, but you need to give yourself time to make decisions rationally on how you truly feel. Give yourself time to understand your self-worth fully, and then choose whether you want to pursue something with them, or go solo.

The truth is, breaking up with someone, or someone breaking up with you, is not as easy as it first seems. It's not as the movies make it out to be. I mean for you, it might be different, but personally, it wasn't what I thought it would be. You believe that breakups are like splitting a KitKat in half, a nice clean break, both of you are happy, you both get the same. Let me tell you what a break up is really like. You imagine splitting a Twix in half, one person always gets a slightly bigger piece, and all that caramel gets stuck to the other part, bits of the biscuit crumble, it's just an all-round mess for everybody

43

involved. You need to set boundaries between you and your ex, understand where they stand. Understand what you both want, talk to one another, this isn't easy, but unless you speak to one another, you're never going to know what those boundaries are. Also, let's quickly talk about talking to your ex for a second. People say, "NEVER TALK TO YOUR EX ONCE YOU HAVE SPLIT UP." You know what that is, bullshit. Let's think; if you don't talk to your ex, you're probably going to spend the next six months thinking "what if." "What if they want to come back to me" "what if they still love me." What if = bullshit overthinking that leads to nothing. There it is, as blunt as it could possibly be. "What if's" get you nowhere. So, if it takes you talking to your ex to understand where to go from there and for you to fully understand what they are feeling without

44

making up magical scenarios in your head, then surely that seems like the logical thing to do...right?

Another thing with splitting up with an ex is the family. This can get pretty sour depending on the reason for the breakup, or you can remain in contact with them. Whenever you're with someone for a while, their family becomes your family, and yours becomes theirs. It becomes harder to imagine yourself without them when you have so many memories with those associated with that person. The thing is here, you can either tackle this by cutting them off and going with the no contact rule (if the relationship has ended sourly), or you remain dropping their Mum the occasional message to meet up for a coffee to discuss what's going on each other's lives. Just because you have split up with someone, does not mean you have split up with their friends and family. They are a part of your life too, and it is okay to remain in contact with them if that is what you want to do to make you happy. However, try to refrain from using them as a mode of trying to get back with your ex, the relationship between their family and you is separate. This can be difficult, and it may take time, but checking in with their family occasionally, isn't that much of a big deal and if it makes you feel better, fuck it, go for it.

No matter how much I've already said it, you are the most important person to you. You need to look after yourself, and if you think your ex will help you achieve that, then go for it. Ignore everybody else, do what makes you happy. Stop being afraid of making the wrong decision because there is no such thing as a wrong decision. Every decision that you make is the right decision for you, at that moment in time. Own that decision and smile.

Chapter Three: Working on your work-life balance

The thing about writing a book, is you think you need to be the expert in the field, which is why very few people end up writing books, even though it is such a cool thing to do!!! You do not need to be an expert, fuck that, do you think I am an expert at killing it? No, but I'm just documenting the journey to try and help anybody that I can on the way, who might be going through the same shit, because guess what, life is tough. A helping hand, a glimpse of guidance is sometimes all we need. But let me tell you, getting a work-life balance is something that I find difficult, even now, I am not going to tell you how to master it, that is down to you, we all have our own shit going on, but I can help you try to clear your head to allow clearer judgment.

Most people are constantly worried about working too much and not living. But how can you live if you have no money? It's like the chicken and egg argument. How can you live life if you do not have the funds to enjoy it? Is it the fun that comes first or the fuel for the fun that needs to be earnt? People get wrapped up in the confusion of trying to enjoy themselves but spend too much time working to be able to do things.

Fuck Susan

You and I both know that there is always someone who appears to be "killing it" more than you, right? Let's call her Susan (apologies to anybody called Susan who is reading this, thank you for buying my book, and I appreciate you). Follow this for a second. You're sat at work, you turn up at 5am to ensure that you get ahead on your day. You secure that client that you have wanted for a long time, continually chasing them, it's been months of work, and you have finally done it. You tell the office how proud you are of yourself, only to hear that *Susan* (who strolls in at 11:36am because she "fancied a lay in") has secured 6 new clients, each with £1,367,372.50 budgets. You crack on with your day, go home in your car, stop at the traffic lights only to see *Susan* pull up next to you in her 2019 plate Range Rover, which makes your 2006 Nissan Micra look a tad out of place. *Susan's* got a mansion in the city, you have 2-bedroom apartment 20 miles outside from any other human existence. Sounds familiar? STOP COMPARING YOURSELF TO SUSAN. Susan has her own shit, it's easy to compare yourself to somebody else who appears to be doing better than you. Truth is, Susan isn't doing any better than you, you're living different lives. Instead of constantly comparing yourself to Susan and how well she is doing for herself, find out how she did it. Use the negative energy that you feel towards Susan, and how she has the latest I-phone and the most beautiful car in the car park, and use it to learn how she got there. People will happily tear somebody down for succeeding, while Susan appears to have the perfect work-life balance (getting a lay in whilst you've been slaving away 6 hours before she even opened her eyes), what you might not know is the groundwork that Susan has put on to be successful in what she's doing. Don't judge and hate Susan, learn from her! Be the next Susan, be better than Susan.

My next tip to you is to leave work at work, leave home at home. Wow, if only it were that easy, right? It's difficult to leave work at work when you're in six different WhatsApp group chats with fifty of your colleagues in discussing when that report is going to get emailed over at 1am, right? It's difficult switching off when you are your own boss, and you can't stop thinking about cash flow or the lack thereof. However, you owe yourself, "you hours." Allow yourself a minimum of 16 "you" tokens a day. Let me explain "You" tokens. Okay, so if I'm telling you the whole way through this book, that you are the driver of your own happiness and you need to put yourself first, it only makes sense that you spend the majority of every single day ensuring that you are: 1. doing something that makes you happy, or 2. making sure that you are okay and well. Let's say you use 8 of your tokens to sleep that leaves you with 8 "you tokens" per day to do whatever the fuck you want with. Have an hour-long bath, read a book, go for a walk, go shopping, Binge watch a whole series on Netflix. Spend those tokens how you want to. My tip for you here, to leave work at work, would be, just before you're about to shut your laptop down for the day and say goodbye to 5,000 emails you received that day, is to write down everything you need to do for tomorrow. Compile a list of every task you didn't quite get finished. That way, you can start your day tomorrow feeling like you have a game plan together and you're not spending the first hour of your day working out where you left off. Tasks will get done faster, you will be more productive, and feel more valued in yourself for getting shit done.

It's okay to say no

Dealing with your bosses demands and being on their beck and call 24/7 is not a long-term fix. By doing this, you are upholding the idea in your boss's mind that you are available all the time for any need they have. Whether that be writing a 3-week report in one day, replying to emails until 5am to be up at 6am to go back into the office, or taking conference calls at 3am because your company has signed a contract with LA and when you're sleeping, they are awake. Stop allowing your instant reaction to be "yes" to everything you're asked to do. Take the extra 30 seconds to think. Is this realistic? Am I going to have enough time to do that? Tell your boss, you might need a little bit more time to do a task if you are unsure, turn to your colleagues for guidance and assistance, that's what they are there for. You are all working on the same team. However, work does not dictate your life. You do not need to continually say yes to tasks and allow them to eat up on "you" time. You will end up running yourself down, and it's not sustainable. Delegate responsibility, ask for more time, or just say no, tell your boss that it's unlikely the task will get finished today. At the end of the day, your boss is a human being also, they will understand that you are not a machine, and if they do not respect that, are you truly happy in your job? Stand up for yourself, respect yourself as a human being, you also need to live a life, your life's purpose is not to slave away for your boss to live a better life. Become your own boss.

Get Done Lists.

If you know me, you'll know I have around 6 to-do - lists. I have a short term to-do-list, long term to-do-list, and the others include things like a reading list. I'm telling you to download an app called "Trello©" (Unpaid product placement, that's how good it is) This app, honestly changed my life. It allows you to see different boards, whether that be teams at work or personal boards for yourself and it is entirely free! There is nothing more satisfying than scribbling things off of a to-do-list. Not only will this help you feel like your day is more productive, but it will also allow you to set short term goals for things you have to get finished - and by when. You will be able to clearly see what you need to do. Trying to get tasks done while you have 100 other things in your mind that you need to remember can be overwhelming, right? WRITE. SHIT. DOWN. Prioritise your daily tasks at work into three categories, (Urgent, Important, and not important). This way, you can clearly see what you must do and what you can allow yourself a little more time on. This is linking to my previous comment about leaving yourself lists for the next day, a task may be less important one day and become urgent another, so through writing these tasks down, and strategising your day, you can knuckle down and get shit done rather than worrying about outstanding jobs you are yet to finish or fear to forget. Getting your shit done within the 8 or so hours you are at work, will hence allow you more time to relax in the evening and give you more "you" tokens to spend. And what's better than an extra hour you can dedicate to watching the next episode of stranger things on Netflix, right?

Work Smarter, not harder

People are always going to tell you to work harder. If you want to succeed, you have to work hard. Bullshit. I'm not saying that hard work isn't necessary for success, because it totally is. However, you should work smarter. Stop tiring yourself out trying to make every conference meeting for 9am when you're out until 12am with clients ensuring they're having a good business meal with you. One way for you to work smarter is to use technology. We have never lived in a time where it is so easy to communicate with other people who are not in the same room as you. Working your strategy for a work-life balance is allowing yourself to live. Say for example you need to take the kids to school for 9am yet you have a conference call at 9:15 (and a 45-minute commute in between). Instead of working ways around doing either of these and feeling like you have either let down your kids or let down your boss, work out ways to compromise. Ask your boss if it is possible for you to Skype into the conference call. Go to your boss with solutions for the "problems" that you have, and you are more likely to get the response you are looking for. For all of you business owners out there, schedule your appointments for your clients around what works for you. People understand that life gets in the way. Instead of cancelling your client, offer a rescheduling appointment. Reschedule Julie for the next day, that's okay, she will understand. Your life comes first. Work comes second. By that, I'm not saying work doesn't need to be done, I'm just saying that the path of your day changes, and rebuilding the work path around that is allowed. Stop beating yourself up, you are killing it. Go you!

Do what YOU love

I was talking to my friend the other day, and she was talking about how she wants to be able to work in a job that she loves so much that she could work at it all the time. Every day. Working in a position that you love is so vital in happiness. How can you be expected the enjoy your evenings away from work if you are continually dreading going back to it the next day, or if you spend your evening complaining to the people you love about how awful your day was? I agree that it is essential you do something you love as a career; however, you must allow for "you" time. In your job, no matter how much you love it every single day, there are still going to be hiccups, things that cause you to stress, maybe you've overbooked your day, perhaps you've put yourself under too much pressure to finish a project. Although you love what you are doing, you still need time to just "no nothing." If you are anything like me, you feel guilty for being unproductive. Sitting around and "doing nothing" seems like a waste of time. But it's the complete opposite. Taking time out of your day, week, or month, to just reflect on how much you have accomplished is so important. Rethink your goals, set new ones. This is so vital in achieving a work-life balance. It allows for you to feel reconnected to knowing yourself, not just your business persona (even though your business persona is a fucking amazing person too). To love yourself and work on yourself, you need to know yourself, and through allowing time for you to do nothing, you learn to understand your emotions and understand how you truly feel. Giving yourself time to love yourself will help improve your headspace, causing you to have higher productivity, and helping you to achieve more. You will smash it, just stick with it.

Achieving a work-life balance isn't easy. These are just some tips to help you deal with the daily struggles you have in your life and how to overcome them. The main note to take away from this chapter is - for you to learn how to balance your work and your life is you need to keep them separate. As simple as it seems, keep your work and home life separate, no matter how much you love your job, you still need time for you. Learn to appreciate yourself, give yourself mini rewards, fuck Susan, and stop comparing yourself to others. You are not like anybody else. You are you. You are killing it. Be proud of who you are and what you have achieved, and you will find yourself a much happier individual. I promise you that.

Chapter 4: Mastering Your Social Life

Okay, let's start this chapter with admitting the fact that we've all done something before just to please someone else. Whether that be going out for drinks with people, you don't really like just to keep your friend happy or going to knitting classes with your Nan to make her day. Beautiful work, making people happy is an amazing feeling. However, where is the line between making other people happy and making yourself miserable. People are so hung up on making other people happy and making other people like them that they lose their sense of self. They forget who they are because they are regularly doing things they do not like, with people they do not really like. I guess you're reading this chapter to try to work out how to get to grips with your social life. I wish I could tell you how to run the perfect social life and to balance it all, but I struggle with this too, in all honesty, most of the time, I will always put others before myself. However, I can share with you little tips and tricks that I use which will enable you to free up some "you" time and allow you to get to know yourself again which will hopefully, in the long run, help you work out who you should be spending time with. Let me start with a fact for you. "You are the average of the five people you spend the most time with." Re-read that sentence and just let that sink in a second.

Think about the five people you spend the most time with. Who are they? What do they bring to your life? Fun? Love? Stories? How do you expect to be the best you can be if you're spending all your time with people who have no ambition? I'm not saying you cut off all your friends. Please don't do that. But distancing yourself from them isn't a problem, taking time to work on yourself with like-minded people, isn't a problem. If your friends see that you are distancing yourself and are constantly pushing for progress, the likelihood is, they are going to want to tag along on the journey, you're going to inspire them to be better people, and what's a better feeling than that?

It's okay to Cancel Plans

We all have those days where you've been run off your feet, and "haven't sat down all day." Sometimes all you want to do is have a long hot bath, put on your pyjamas, watch a movie, and go to bed by 7pm. We've all been there, and that's okay. We all cancel plans, whether it be going to the bar with your friends for a drink, or going to dinner with the parents of your significant other, we have all cancelled plans at some point in our lives. There is no need to feel guilty for bailing, people will understand. Yeah, sure they might be a little pissed off that you do not want to go with them to see the new Star Wars movie (even though you've never seen the previous 6), but they will forgive you. Treat yourself with the utmost respect, if you need an early night because you are feeling run down, give it to yourself. If you're anything like me, you have plans cancelled on you all the time! Dates, Dinners, Bingo Games, people bail all the time, but you get over it, right? It's okay to make plans with yourself, realistically, you're not going to bail on yourself, are you? So, cancel that unwanted dinner, get your slippers on and settle down and read a good book (do not put this down and pick up another book, this is the good book I am referring to). The moment that you stop yourself getting mad at people bailing is the moment that people respect you more as an understanding person. Understand that people have reasons for bailing, and that is okay. You can bail, they can bail. Just reach out and ask them if they are okay, show them you still care, rather than showing them you're frustrated with them.

Your Grand Library

I'm going to introduce to you another analogy that might help you visualise your social life differently, so that it seems more manageable, especially if you have a busy social life. Okay, picture this, you're stood on the bottom floor of this grand library. The most magnificent library you've ever seen. There are multiple floors, each containing hundreds of books. If you've ever seen Shrek, think of the potion room in the Fairy Godmothers House. That scale. This library is vast, and each floor in this library is dedicated to an aspect of your life.

So, you're on the ground floor, and your level guide looks something like this (albeit, yours might look different, everybody's is different):

Level 1: Family &

Level 2: Friends

Level 3: Relationships

Level 4: Education

Level 5: Work

Level 6: Memories

Level 7: Hobbies

So you walk up the stairs to level 1, and you see hundreds of books, each one titled with a member of your family. Now, by taking one of these books off the shelf and reading it for a while, that symbolises you going and spending time with that individual. So, say for example you take off the book that is your Mum, you taking her shopping for a couple hours is you reading a few pages of her book. When you're done, you just place the book on the shelf to go back into another time. Then you can go to another level to open another book and spend some time reading it. With mastering your social life, you can open a book, for example, going for dinner with your friend, and place them back on the shelf. If you look at your social plans as books that can be placed on shelves, you will be able to plan your time more effectively because it will stop you from double-booking and overworking yourself. What happens when you read too much at one time? You get tired, right? And you don't want to have to read two books at the same time because you told two of your characters in these books that you'd spend some time with them. Take your time to read your books and work out a suitable plan that works for you and the characters in your book to ensure that you have time to understand your own book too.

Part of managing your social life includes managing your daily life too. You need to work out how to get your shit together before you can even consider planning your social life. Being busy can either make you or break you. Don't get me wrong, I know what it's like to be busy like you're spinning 700 plates at once. You drop one, and it seems like the end of the world, but the other plates are still standing. Don't address all your focus to the one that fell. Plates will fall, and that's okay, but do not let all your other plates fall because you are caught up on the broken one and forget to spin the rest. Sticking with the plate spinning analogy for a moment, you can use it to understand priority. Some plates are going to need more spinning than others. Maybe they're more substantial, or bigger, these plates are going to need more attention, but you still need to spin the smaller plates. Take me for example, I have three jobs, I regularly go to the gym, I am building my portfolio for a tattooing apprenticeship, I dance, and I am studying psychology at Uni, just to name a few of the things I am doing in my life. My most significant plates that need spinning at the moment is finishing my degree and keeping up to date with my work. But this doesn't mean I ignore giving attention to my friends and working out. It's all about organising your time. Everybody has the same 24 hours in the day, it's how you spend it that counts.

An Amateurs Guide to: Killing It

Get a diary

Personally, I have a physical diary that I carry around everywhere with me. I'm telling you, it's a lifesaver. You need to write things down as soon as you make the plan, otherwise, you end up in those awkward moments of double or even triple booking yourself. With a diary, everything is laid out exactly how you want it, so you can see it. I'm not saying it needs to be neat and tidy, sometimes it looks like a 5-year-old has got hold of mine. But at least all the information for your day is in one place, it feels incredible.

Allow time for travel

This is something that I forget most of the time. The day that someone develops a time machine will be the best day of my life. When you're planning out your day, make sure that you allocate time to get wherever you need to be. There's no point saying you'll meet a friend at 5 when you finish work at 5, and they live 40 minutes away. Be realistic with your time, feeling like you're late all the time will put you under unnecessary strain.

10-minute planning

Take 10 minutes when you start to feel overwhelmed to plan precisely what you need to get done. Chunk it into bitesize pieces, and you'll get there. It takes 10 minutes at the start of your day to plan out exactly what you need to get done and I can promise you, your day will be a lot more productive than if you constantly guess what you should do, and keep postponing things for the next day (which never actually get done, we've all been there).

Allow yourself downtime

It's so easy to get rolled up in pleasing everybody and making sure that you've divided your time to complete every task you've set for that day. You need to allocate yourself downtime. Time for yourself. As cliché as it sounds, it's the most essential time, and I find this just as difficult, it's not easy. Even if it's that 20-minute bath at the end of the day, or the hour in the morning that you want to catch up on planet earth or read your book, plan time for yourself to just relax and let your mind run. Try not to feel guilty for not doing something all the time. Your brain may still run wild but allow it to happen. You will learn to appreciate yourself more, love yourself more, and you will thank yourself for giving yourself the attention that you provide for other people.

An Amateurs Guide to: Killing It

At the end of the day, you need to ensure that you are happy. That is the message that I'm trying to get across, and looking after your social life and planning "you" time, is so crucial in that.

Chapter Five: Overcoming Procrastination

Welcome, fellow procrastinator. If you are anything like myself, you are a master of finding other things to do rather than getting the work done. Whether that be scrolling through social media, watching thousands of hours on youtube trying to find out how the crochet yourself a jumper, or learning how to care for a pet Emu. How are us procrastinators ever expected to get shit done when there are so many more exciting options. Revise for an exam or teach your dog his left and right? I know which one I would choose. But is there a way to "crack" procrastination? Imagine how much more productive you could be if you didn't procrastinate. I wish I could sit here as I am writing this and tell you how to turn your procrastination into productivity and transform your brain to work more efficiently. However, I can't. I especially cannot tell you how to solve your procrastination problems as a procrastinator myself (mainly because chapter nine is about not being a hypocrite). However, what I can do for you is give you tips on how to tame your procrastination mane, and keep it at bay.

Your Procrastination Pet

First of all, what is procrastination? I'm not going to give you an Oxford Dictionary definition that you'll most probably skip over. Let me explain procrastination to you, in the only way that I can explain anything. Analogies. If you're not bored of the analogies yet, then hopefully you will find this one interesting. See, procrastination is like a new puppy (in your brain), and productivity is the owner. The "productive you" can go about tasks, running errands, doing assignments, going to work, all things like that. Your "procrastination pet" on the other hand, loves attention. Sometimes you can give your procrastination pet little bursts of attention, whether that be going for a walk, or scrolling through Facebook every now and again. But what you didn't know when you purchased your procrastination pet is, the more attention he gets, the more he wants. He will not stop continually bothering your productivity, hounding for longer walks and more food. Sometimes your productive mind caves into the demands of the procrastination pet, and this is when you end up getting into a rapid circle of unproductively. You need to learn to sometimes lock your procrastination pet up in a cage. Just like a new puppy, when you first lock them up in the cage, they do not stop crying, doing everything they can to get your attention. Stay strong. A well-trained procrastination pet takes taming, do not let them rule your life. You are the owner. Not the pet.

Stop feeling guilty.

Stop making yourself feel guilty for procrastinating. Procrastination is okay, the more you punish yourself for it, the more you are going to stress yourself out. Stressing yourself out is going to lead to you feeling overwhelmed. Your overwhelming feeling is going to lead to nothing but negative thoughts, and you're more likely going to procrastinate more to protect yourself from addressing the problem. So, to stop yourself feeling stressed out, do not punish yourself for your mind wondering. If you apply this tip to your everyday life, you're going to feel more in control of your actions, which will allow your head and your thoughts to be clearer.

PLAN AHEAD

With things like exams, work reports, and deadlines in general, the key to helping feed your "procrastination pet" is to plan ahead. Say you have an exam in two weeks, work out the amount of revision you need to do daily and allow yourself to plan procrastination time, refer to tip number one and do not feel guilty procrastinating, just give yourself time to. For example, you need to read a book chapter, allow yourself to read a page, then go and do something that you want to do, whether that be to find your house on google earth and work out how many steps it would take you to walk from your front door to the Great Wall of China, or watching a youtube video. Don't schedule yourself unrealistic tasks. Your procrastination pet LOVES it when you are unrealistic. You're basically letting him have free roam, you let him out of the cage. There is nothing more that your procrastination pet loves more than no time schedule. When you stop forward planning, this only leads to one thing. Last minute panic. Whether it's trying to write a dissertation in a night or trying to pull together four weeks of work into four hours, not only will your brain go into overload, the quality of that work, is more likely to not be the best it could be. Note here, I'm saying likely, some people work better under strict time constraints, but don't use this as an excuse. Try not to convince yourself that you work better under pressure when you know all it's going to really do is cause you significant stress. It's not worth it. Plan ahead, make little milestones, and allow yourself procrastination time.

Why are you Procrastinating?

Try to address the task at hand and work out why you are procrastinating. Now we get the idea that sometimes you have to do things you don't really want to do. However, if you are finding yourself procrastinating a lot of the time, maybe it's time to re-evaluate the tasks you are procrastinating and work out why you are continually trying to get away with not completing it. Is it because you do not like the task itself? If this is the case, then you need to understand if the job is going to benefit you in any way. For example, there is nothing I procrastinate more on that writing my University assignments, and yeah, I really don't like writing 2,000-word essays every week. However, I know that it will benefit the bigger picture. Take time to stand back and look at whether it is worth you finishing those small (which seem huge) tasks to achieve the reward in the long run. Looking at the grand scheme of things will help you to focus your thoughts on achieving your goals and therefore stop procrastinating as much because you see the vision of success at the end of it.

An Amateurs Guide to: Killing It

Eliminate Distractions

We all know the temptation of distractions. Our phones being the main one. You just pick up your phone for two minutes, the next thing you know two days have passed, and you haven't moved, right? Or you wish to clear one more level on candy crush which takes you all five lives and a solid four hours to complete. We've all been there. Another way to overcome procrastination would be to eliminate all distractions from your view. Turn your phone off, pause your Netflix series, turn the TV off. Set milestone goals with the task you have to complete and reward yourself with distractions. By that I mean write a couple hundred words of your essay, read one chapter of that book, reply to those emails, and then reward yourself with ten minutes of instagram scrolling or one episode of Ru Pauls Drag Race (Highly recommend this series by the way). The more time you've allowed yourself to do the

84

task (by planning ahead) the more often your distraction breaks can be.

Monkey See Monkey Do

Find yourself someone who has already completed the task that you are trying to achieve. I don't mean copy their work, I mean copy their approach to the work. Ask them what they did to get the job done in time, and try that. Say it's something more significant than a University essay, say you're writing up your first business plan. Read successful business owners autobiographies, work out their approach to situations like this. Model success.

We all procrastinate, and you know what, that's okay. Things will get one when they need to get done, deadlines will get met (even if it is last minute). Use these tips and master a way that works for you. What worked for me, might not work for you, and that is also okay, believe in yourself that you can complete

the task at hand, and you will, every time.

Chapter Six: Reconnecting with Happiness

Firstly, let's clear something up, I am not trying to tell you how to live your life. You could be reading this thinking, at 21 years old, I have no life experience to be telling you how to be happy. And you would be correct, I do not have the life experience of someone who is 60. However, I know for a fact there are unhappy 60 years old, happiness is something that affects every single one of us yet is something that so many of us overlook every single day. Without even realising it. We all want to be happy, right? We become so consumed in our daily lives that we forget to have fun. We forget to laugh. This whole book aims to show you that life isn't always about being a professional, its about experience. It's about enjoyment, laughter, and fun. Memories are made through laughter. Here we are going to talk about how to reconnect yourself back to the things in your life that give you nothing but pure enjoyment. Do something for yourself. I'll help you to rediscover that happiness that is within you.

Discover what makes you happy

Try new things, meet new people, work out what makes you happiest. Write down everything that you do in your life and highlight the things that make you happy. By writing down everything you do, you'll be able to clearly see if there is more you can be doing to make yourself happy. By seeing it blatantly in front of you, you will stop feeling guilty for having fun. This is because most of us go around thinking we have no time for fun. Stop kidding yourself. If you have become consumed by being busy, are you really going to be able to tell if you are having fun? All you see are tasks that need completing. The things that you used to love become invisible because you're "too busy" to notice they're missing. Take the time to work out what it is that truly gives you nothing but pure enjoyment, whether that be reading a book or going bungee jumping. Do something for you!

Appreciate your surroundings

Things get in the way of allowing you to live your life. I understand that. "If I could just lose weight… I would be happy" "If I could just get a promotion… I would be happy" "If I could just find the love of my life… I would be happy". Things get in the way. And people have bad days. Yes. However, people become so fixed on what they *want* to make them happy that they ignore the peripheral. Say for example you want to get a promotion at work, get more money, sure that'll make you happy...right? You become so focused. Imagine looking through a telescope, you can see yourself with that promotion, you feel it. Thing is, when you're walking towards your goal looking through a telescope, you can't see what is happening around you. Next thing you know you've stepped into the main road because all your eyes are fixed on is "earning more money." Then people get disheartened when matters knock them off course. The cars knock them down, relationship problems, losing friendships all because that person wants that money to make them happy. I'm not saying do not focus on your goal, you should, however, keep your peripheral open and do not ignore everything around you that previously made you happy, to get to one thing that you *need* to make you happier. There will be people who will help you build bridges over those roads, and you'll probably end up getting there faster by not shutting them out.

An Amateurs Guide to: Killing It

Create your own energy

A lot of people always say to me, "Shannon, you're always so full of energy... how" or "Shannon it's 1am, you've just finished work, how are you still singing and dancing". It is down to one thing. One phrase that my Dad once told me that has resonated with me more than I think even he realised. "The power plant doesn't have energy, it generates and transforms energy." People regularly make excuses as to why they spend their lives feeling fatigued. "I didn't get enough sleep last night" "I haven't eaten today" "I'm just having a bad day." Don't get me wrong, I completely understand that those things contribute to your energy levels, and we all have bad days. But how much energy does it take to laugh? If you're having a bad day, watch a 10-second funny cat video, laugh with a friend, do something that makes you smile, even for a split second. I can promise you, it will change your day, even if it is for a short period of time. Even if you force that smile on your face with absolutely everything that it takes, do you know how difficult it is to still feel down when you're smiling?

Reconnect

Think of it this way, when your phone is dying, what do you do? You plug it in, right? Sometimes you need to just plug yourself back into what makes you happy. So many people get wound up in constantly pleasing other people, myself sometimes included, it's easy to lose touch in what you love. But take a moment to plug yourself back into what makes you happy. Take the time to make that phone call with your friend that you haven't spoken to in a few weeks, ring your mum and ask her how her day is going. Something so small can make such a significant difference.

An Amateurs Guide to: Killing It

On the Bright-side

So, let me tell you a story. I went to Alicante a couple years back with my friends and on the way home our flight got cancelled. Long story short, we ended up being stranded for three days waiting for a return flight back to the UK. As you can imagine, everybody is tired, wound up, and negative emotions towards this particular airline were running high. My friend turns to me and introduces me to a game called "on the bright side." In this game, you take time to appreciate little things that are good in that moment. So, we start listing things, "on the bright side, we are not cold" "on the bright side, we all have each other" "on the bright side, we have just had an amazing holiday." I'm not kidding you when I say that it instantly improved our mood, we ended up laughing rather than crying. This game may sound like something to just pass the time; however, it grounds you, makes you realise that there is so much around you that you can be grateful for. It makes the negative situation seem insignificant because you'll be surprised by how much is going on around you that you can appreciate and half the time take for granted. I invite you to play this game because it's now my "go-to" in any bad situation!

Take breaks from Social Media

Scrolling through your phone might make you happy. That might be the time you take for yourself to relax. That's okay. However, social media can become draining and end up making you feel worse in the long run, believe it or not. Now, social media is an amazing platform, however, having a break from constantly trying to keep up with everybody, can make you feel happier. The instant relief you get from having genuine downtime for yourself, and nobody else can be so rewarding, to you and your mental health. Deleting these apps from your phone every once in a while will help you disconnect yourself from your phone and will cause you to draw attention to other things that you appreciate in life that you may have been overlooking. Take a break from social media, and go and spend a day with your loved ones, go and discover a new hobby, go and take a long walk. Your phone does not define you, appreciate the world around you, take it in.

Meditate

Meditation is another thing that can seriously help your overall happiness. I don't mean sitting like a pretzel humming away to some zen music. Even taking 2 minutes to just focus on your breathing, you can dramatically improve your state of mind, and therefore, your happiness levels. Attacking your day with a clear mind is inevitably going to ensure you have a more positive day than if you take on tasks with clouded judgement. Every morning when you wake up, allow yourself

2 minutes to just lay and focus on your breathing. Exhaling and inhaling slowly. Start your day calm rather than frantic. Meditation takes practice, do not give up if the first time you take 2 minutes you cannot fully relax, that's okay. Observe the emotions you are feeling and truly understand them. Understand how and why you're feeling the way that you are. Even through doing this, you're evaluating your emotions and therefore taking time to focus on yourself. The more you meditate, the easier you will find it to fully relax your mind and truly let go. Stick with it, because that feeling is like nothing I've experienced before.

People are like The SimsTM

So, remember The Sims™, the absolute peak of childhood, and if you have never heard of it, then I recommend that you go straight to a game store and get on it (you need to get the original one before any expansion packs, learned that the hard way). Okay, so, when your Sim was hungry, you instructed it to go and make dinner, right? When you Sim was lonely, you'd force them on dates, right? When your Sim was unhappy, you didn't just ignore it, because otherwise you'd end up walking around in that zombie-like-state and your Sim would eventually refuse to do anything you wanted it to, right? So why would you ignore your own happiness? Take a leaf from the Sims, you need to address the fact that you may be unhappy, the fact that your happiness meter might be running low. It doesn't mean its destine to stay low forever, your Sim wasn't unhappy forever. You told *them* to listen to music or sleep or chat with friends. So, why would you punish yourself for being unhappy? Go and instruct yourself and your inner Sim to enjoy themselves! Fill your happiness meter back up and stop walking like a zombie!

An Amateurs Guide to: Killing It

Write Shit Down

I've said it before, and I'll repeat it but writing things down really does help. My advice here to you would be to get a diary, throw it back to primary school days when you used to write down your top ten crush list. A journal allows you to write down how you are feeling and keep track of it. Not only will it let you get out all of your frustrations without hurting anybody around you, it is so beneficial to look back into the past. You can turn back to days when you were feeling negative, and almost coach yourself on how you got through that time. Writing things down will help you to work out game plans to progress forward, and it will allow you to understand yourself. When I'm feeling a certain way about something, I usually write blogs on it, it's a way of conveying emotion into something that is affecting you at that moment. So, my "overcoming overwhelm" blog, I wrote while I was starting to feel overwhelmed. Not only does it allow me to help others, but I also coach myself through my emotions by writing down ways to overcome these feelings. Taking a leaf out of my own book, effectively, Get yourself a diary or open a word document, and start writing shit down.

Sleep is SO important

Okay, my final tip for you to reconnect with happiness is as simple as sleeping. This is a massive one for me, I understand that things get in the way and eight hours of sleep a night isn't always possible. Sometimes you need to finish that Netflix series, sometimes you need to go and meet your Auntie's new dog, life gets in the way of sleep. However, let me tell you one thing. NAPS ARE SO UNDERRATED. Take power naps. 20-minute power naps throughout the day will allow you to feel recharged. However, the same rules apply to napping as those that apply to meditating. It takes practice. You might be thinking, napping takes practice, what is she talking about.

Hear me out, when you wake up from a nap and feel more tired? That's because your body is not used to it, the more you power nap, the easier it gets and the more charged you feel when you wake up. Feeling charged will increase your happiness.

I hope that you can implement these small pointers to reconnect with happiness. You are in control of your emotions (even if you feel like sometimes you just "feel sad"). Your thoughts control your feelings, and your thoughts can be changed a heartbeat. Pick your head up, shake yourself off, make a game plan, smile, and kill it.

Chapter Seven: Improving your self-esteem

The feeling of not being good enough is one that can kill. Looking in the mirror and seeing an abundance of insecurities and imperfection. That thought of "why am I not good enough" follows you around, consuming your thoughts, for every second of every day. You become so absorbed by the power of your mind that you believe what you see. You say to yourself if I could just lose a few pounds or if my lips could be just that little bit bigger, maybe I would have been good enough. You strive for the look of perfection, for that approval of one person, when in real fact, you're losing respect for yourself. You're building a reputation for the shell of the person you are.

It's safe to say, we all go through stages of having low self-esteem. It's something that affects everybody, and many things contribute to it. You're always going to be over critical of yourself, don't punish yourself for it, everybody does it. Everybody looks at themselves and says, "if I could just do this" or "if I could just be like them." But you are the most important person to you. The only opinion that truly matters when you are evaluating yourself is your own. Everybody is different, and everybody has personal qualities. You might be a great listener, you might be an amazing friend, a skilled gymnast, whatever it is, everybody has things that they are good at. So many people say to me, "you do so much, and I'm not doing anything." Rule number one to improving your self-esteem is STOP COMPARING YOURSELF TO OTHER PEOPLE. Your journey is personal, what you choose to do in your life is entirely up to you, it really doesn't matter what anybody else is doing. So they might have a higher paid job than you, but they may not have the family you have. They might have a really nice car, but you have a partner that loves you. People will most probably look at you too and compare themselves to you. Stop overlooking what you have because you're in need for more. Appreciate every person in your life, appreciate everything that happens in your life because we all have flaws, and we all have qualities, stop replacing your qualities with flaws.

When you see another girl on Instagram, videoing themselves, posing, the first thing we do is shoot them down. "Oh, she must love herself" "she's so vain." Truth is, those girls are the ones who have their shit together the most. Those girls love the most important person the most, themselves. Those girls are what I and many others strive to be, not because they are beautiful (and they are) but because they have the most amount of pride in who they are, something we all strive to have.

Your mental health is so vitally important, especially when it comes to your self-esteem; therefore, you need to care for it just as much as you care for your physical health. Stress, anxiety, fear, sadness, all of these emotions contribute and have a significant influence on your mental health and hence your self-esteem. Therefore if you just overlook them, it will become increasingly difficult to increase your self-esteem. If you're feeling overwhelmed, take a step back, and just breathe, work out what is making you feel that way. If you're feeling stressed, stop what you're doing, ask yourself, why are you stressed?

Instead of continually looking for the approval of others, learn to love yourself first. Once you realise how much of a beautiful person you are, only then will it highlight in others. You will adjust your time to helping others to cure their insecurities instead of being consumed by your own. It may be a long journey, but we have nothing but time. Take a deep breath, smile, and show the world how fucking amazing you are.

Appreciate yourself

We are so self critical of ourselves, in everything we do. Whether that be body goals, job goals, money goals, anything, we are constantly striving for more. Stop putting yourself down because you're not like somebody else. You are your own person, and you are amazingly perfect, do not let yourself tell you otherwise. Write down 5 things that you genuinely like about yourself (if anybody did this is social studies, they'll know how amazing you felt after it), take five minutes to appreciate yourself and appreciate what you love about yourself.

1. _____

2. _____

3. _____

4. _____

5. _____

Everybody makes mistakes

You're not the only person in the entire world to make a mistake. We make mistakes all the time, it's natural. Sometimes they're big mistakes, sometimes small. Sometimes they'll change your mood, sometimes they'll change your future, but you're only human. People make mistakes, and none of us are perfect. Acknowledge the fact that you fucked up, but try not to dwell on it, after all, this may seem like a mistake now but may open the door to an opportunity down the line. Mistakes are okay. Fuck ups are okay, apologise, and move on. Fixating your energy on the error, doesn't fix it, but dealing with the consequences and owning that decision, does. Focus on what you can change rather than what you can't. Identify the issues at hand and create a plan to fix them.

Spend time doing things that make you happy

Take time for yourself, and do things that you love. Schedule in time to love yourself, allow yourself to fully relax in whatever that may be. Have a long hot bath, go for a walk, read a book, watch a Netflix series, go for dinner, do something that makes you happy. Take a break from your day to day life, step back from the responsibilities that you face every day and give yourself some well deserved "you" time.

Give yourself a round of applause

Let me tell you a story, when I was 18, for my birthday my Dad bought me tickets for a Tony Robbins event, Unleash the Power Within (Thank You Dad). Now, this weekend was pretty intense; however, there was one part of it that has stuck in my memory ever since. He spoke about giving yourself recognition, where recognition is due. So, when you complete daily task goals that you set yourself, give yourself a round of applause. This may sound so stupid, but I promise you, it's incredible. Finish that book? Give yourself a round of applause. Made that playlist you've been meaning to for months? Give yourself a good old clap. Got out of bed when you really didn't want to? Connect those hands like you've never connected them before. By giving yourself a round of applause when you complete a task, you are drawing attention to the fact that you've finished something you set out to do. This will, in time, make you feel better about yourself because you will feel like you're actually getting shit done.

Surround yourself with the right people

Positive Pals will help with your self-esteem. If you are always hanging around negative nelly's, guess what, your vibe isn't gonna be very positive. YOUR VIBE ATTRACTS YOUR TRIBE. If you hang around with positive people, who all share a similar outlook on life as you do, you will find yourself adopting their perspective. We've all had it where you'll be hanging out with one specific person for a long time, and you'll start to adapt their mannerisms right? You might start talking like them, or saying things they say, your mind works the same way. It feeds off the energy of the people you are around. You are a combination of the top five people you spend time with. I've said it before in this book, and I'll repeat it because it is so true. I'm not saying ditch the people who are negative in your life, after all, Winnie the Pooh remained friends with Eeyore, right? I'm just saying focus your time on the people that have the same outlook as you do. This will also help you to be a shoulder to lean on for your friends who are more negatively driven. If they see you becoming more positive in your outlook, they are more likely to come to you for help and advice. This has two advantages. You will bring your friends up with you in your positive mindset, and change the way they think about themselves and the world too, and to know that you are someone that other people can rely on, will also massively boost your self-esteem, win-win.

Treat yourself

Another way of appreciating yourself is to treat yourself. Give yourself what you deserve. Whether that be buying yourself some new trainers because you got through a really tough day, or something more extravagant like booking yourself a getaway trip to Rome to indulge in some "Me time" while sipping wine and dipping in thermal baths. It's good to give yourself gifts every now and again to reward yourself, you're still here, and you've survived every single one of your bad days, now, if that doesn't deserve getting yourself a gift, I don't know what does.

Improving your self esteem will take time, and a lot of work, things will not change overnight, you will not meditate for three minutes and all of a sudden completely love yourself and feel completely different on your outlook towards life (I mean, if you do, I commend you, and that's amazing). Be patient, self-love will come over time, and you can't fix in days the damage that occurred over years. Stick with it, you're doing an amazing job.

An Amateurs Guide to: Killing It

Chapter Eight: Understanding it's okay not to be okay

I'm going to try and write this chapter in the most unpatronising way that I can. I know how it feels to not be okay and have someone try and tell you to just "smile." I'm not trying to patronise you, but when I say that everything will be okay eventually, I mean it. Events will get in the way of you being the best person you can be. That's okay, and not every day will be productive. That's also okay. Sometimes you'll cry over stupid things. That's okay. It doesn't mean you have any less self-worth. You are still killing it every day. You are still here, still fighting. People will piss you off, that's life, but pick yourself up, shake yourself off and keep going on the journey towards your goals. You're allowed to take breaks when you're taking the long road to success. A car can't get to the destination without fuel stops. Take care of yourself along the way. One of the main problems I face is thinking that I to be positive all the time, but it's only recently that I've accepted that not always being okay, is also okay. Having down days are allowed. You owe yourself them. You owe yourself time to recuperate your thoughts and regenerate the energy you have within, there is no rush.

Setbacks are not failures

We all have setbacks, one moment you're okay, the next minute you can't stop crying, we all get that feeling. I'm going to be honest with you, just before I started to get to work on writing this chapter, I had a setback. You know the feeling when you try on that one dress or shirt that you ordered online, and it's just the most unflattering piece of clothing you've ever tried on? Yeah, that was me this morning. Also, note to self, DIY bleaching your hair is always a bad idea and should never be attempted (I'm currently sat here with some florescent orange roots). So, yeah I haven't had a great morning, and to you reading this, it might seem insignificant, and to me, now, this seems so irrelevant, yet at the time you convince yourself that it's the end of the world. But it's not until a few hours have passed that you realise that your meltdown is no longer as significant as you first thought. It will always get better, and it's okay to have bad mornings. Meltdowns are moments that you'll look back on and go "that was tough, and I got through it" or "What the fuck was that about?", both have positive outcomes. You look back on it and realise how tough it was, and you observe how much you've grown since and how much of a stronger person you are, or you look back at it and realise that it was over something so stupid that it's laughable, and you laugh away at it, tell your friends about the shit morning you've had, laughter is just as positive as learning. Either way, you got this, you can get through this, and you've survived 100% of your bad days, so what's one more to add to the journey? Take a moment to breathe, everything will always be okay.

Stay Focused

Try to keep your thoughts focused on your end goal, just because you're having a bad day, a bad week, a bad year, do not abandon your plans, simply postpone them. Write them down, keep the thought there, address it later, that's okay. Dealing with things when you are in a better state of mind is worth so much more than fulfilling a task when your head is in the wrong place. Keep your heart strong, keep your passion alive, and do what makes you happy. This all links back to how I keep going on about writing things down. It is so important to get your ideas down on paper because then they go from dreams to goals. But we'll address that later on in the changing 'if' to 'when' chapter so sit tight.

So, what do you do, if you don't feel okay? Here are some tips on what to do in these situations, because we all know it's not easy.

Do something that makes you happy

Linking with my reconnecting with happiness chapter, do something that makes you feel good, and don't feel guilty about it. Some of the things that make you happy, might not be what makes other people happy, but it's not about them. Watching Netflix, eating Ice Cream, listening to music. Take time to yourself and to allow yourself to fully immerse yourself in calmness and tranquility.

Change your environment

Not feeling okay, is often linked to the situation you're in. So, take yourself out of the environment that is making you feel this way, even if it is temporary. Take yourself to a safe space, somewhere that makes you feel happy. For me, it's my bedroom. However, shutting yourself into your own space might not be the best thing for you. Go to a friends house, go for a walk down the street, just remove yourself from the situation that is making you feel unhappy. This quickly removes what could be whirlpool forming in your mind and allows you to rationalist your thoughts.

An Amateurs Guide to: Killing It

Don't suffer in silence

When you're feeling overwhelmed, it is vital to talk to somebody about it, and I know how difficult that can be. Reaching out for help is seemingly the hardest step to take when you're not feeling okay. However, asking for help from someone helps you to rationalise your thoughts. I've had many a day where I'm feeling frantically overwhelmed, but just speaking to somebody about it, really clears my head, and settles my mind. Simple conversations can be life-changing. From a distance, your drowning might look like waving. But speak up, shout for help, and help will come for you. Do not feel like you're burdening other people with your own issues, because this is so far from the truth. No problem is too small to ask for help, remember that. Talk to someone you trust, a friend, a family member, anyone, and if that is seeming too tricky, in the back page of this book, you'll find numbers of helplines which can help you when you are not feeling okay and are not ready to ask for help from someone you know.

You can change at ANY moment

You do not need to wait for a new day, a new week or a new year. You can change at any point, there is no 'right time' for change, and sometimes when you assess why you are not feeling okay, you realise that it is time for a change. However, don't take this as you have to change. You don't. You don't need to become a "brand new you" to change, you are you. You need to accept that sometimes you are sad. This whole journey is yours entirely.

You're not alone

When you fall into the rabbit hole of not feeling okay, it becomes very easy to believe that you're the only person that's in that hole because it's so dark, you can't see anybody else. It's so easy to think that everybody else has their lives together and you're not 'as good as them.' What a shit statement. Just remember, it is SO easy to post on social media about your happiness and build a false facade on your life. Don't feel like you're the only person who is struggling because everybody on your instagram feed is having a great time. Everybody is struggling in one way or another, they just might not show it. Don't feel like you need to continually compare yourself to others.

Everything is so much more shit when you're hungover

I've been there. Thinking that hardcore drinking is the way to fix your problem, and it probably does, for the night. However, that next morning when you wake up, holy shit it's gonna feel like a mistake. The anxiety that calmed down after that second bottle of wine will definitely hit you full force the next day, and it's so not worth it. Alcohol will seem like your friend, but I promise you, it's really not. Take a bath and an early night. Sometimes, life can be a real shit show, but you are still breathing, you are okay, you will be okay eventually. Pain is only temporary. Reach out for help.

Being sad, feeling down, and not being okay is not an issue. You are the most important person to you, and therefore you should care about yourself more than you care about anybody else. Just like when you're on an aeroplane, and they make that safety announcement and say "fit your own oxygen mask before attempting to help fit anybody else's." How are you expected to help anybody else when you're restricting yourself of oxygen. You need to make sure you take care of yourself before you try and help others because otherwise, you are just putting yourself at risk of oxygen starvation. What a lot of people do, is not even realise the oxygen mask is in front of them. They are so blissfully unaware that they are not okay because they cannot see the oxygen thinning. They've convinced themselves they are okay when in real fact, they are secretly suffocating, and the thing that is killing them is the *thought* that they are okay when they're not. To fit their oxygen mask, the first thing they need to do admit to themselves that there is a problem. The same goes for you, if you are struggling, the first step to securing that mask is acknowledging that you're not okay. The moment you realise that something is wrong is the moment you reach for it.

Sticking with the oxygen mask analogy for a moment. Say you've been suffocating for some time now, your vision is hazed, you start choking, and you get the feeling that you're not going to make it. You then see the oxygen mask hanging in front of you. You grab it and start breathing frantically, expecting the oxygen to just flood back into your body straight away, but when you've been suffocating for so long, instant full recovery isn't realistic. It takes time for your body to readjust to the fact that you're now trying to save it. Reaching out for help might not cause you to feel okay straight away, but it doesn't mean that your body hasn't already slowly started healing itself. Stick with the idea that 'this will eventually help me, and I will get better,' and you will begin to regain your vision and see the route for where the problem is. Only then can you clearly see what was restricting your oxygen in the first place, and from there you can work on fixing that issue.

Not being okay, is not a sign of weakness, it's a sign of strength. To "not be okay" means you have admitted the fact you aren't alright, which is the first step in becoming okay again. I said it at the beginning of this chapter, and I'll say it again, YOU HAVE SURVIVED 100% OF YOUR BAD DAYS. If that isn't something to be proud of, I don't know what is!

An Amateurs Guide to: Killing It

Chapter Nine: Don't be a hypocrite

Stop thinking that you need to abide by other people's rules and do what they tell you to do. This is how most people fall into the hypocrite category. They'll say one thing and then as soon as their friend says something that conflicts their beliefs, they'll jump on the bandwagon to preserve their friendship. But surely your friend will respect the difference in opinion, not everybody will agree with you. You'll lose touch with people over your journey in life, and that is okay, you must grow with yourself, those who want to grow with you are welcome them on the journey, but you do not need to change your path because of the way other people think.

Experience

Unless you've experienced something, reserve your opinion. Do not try to tell people how to live their lives and give them people life advice you can't follow yourself. This is the crucial part of hypocrisy, people are quick to criticise how others are reacting to situations when they have no idea what they are going through. Support people who need help rather than trying to "fix" them and offer them a shoulder to lean on rather than criticising them for the way they are.

Bitching

Stop bitching. Plain and straightforward, bitching about people behind their back is a key example of being a hypocrite. "School playground bitching" is a game often played by people who are just trying to cause drama. Don't get dragged into that. Don't be consumed by negative energy. It's boring, it's draining, and it's just unnecessary. People will trust you if you are a reliable person who won't slag them off? Obviously…right? Look at the situation from other peoples perspective and honestly try to gauge how they are feeling. Put yourself in someone else shoes and try to understand how they are feeling, instead of bitching about them. They are no 'less' of a person than you are, so empathise with them, and don't talk down to people. Empathising will help you to think before you speak, which inevitably will stop you from making hypocritical comments.

Follow your own advice

Take me, for example, through-out this whole book, I'm talking about writing things down in a diary, because I do that, and it works for quieting my mind from the unnecessary ambience. I'm not spouting out bullshit for you to read because I think it's interesting content, I'm writing this to hopefully inspire you and to help you to find a way to make your life that little bit easier. But you need to stick with your own advice and take a leaf out of your own book, so I'm not writing this whole book on bullshit, because everything I'm telling you about, works for me. It might not be your thing, and that's okay, but this is what I'm trying to get at. Following your own advice, staying active with your personal opinion and advice and not letting other peoples opinions sway you,

Stay Grounded

Nobody is perfect, and people fuck things up. But it is vital to stay grounded. I continuously talk about growing and if people aren't willing to grow with you, then leave them behind, but I don't mean criticise them. Hypocrites are the first to call out people on mistakes they've already made. People may just be in a different stage in their life, and that's okay. There's no need to put someone down to make yourself feel better.

This is a short chapter, but it's simple. We have all been hypocrites in the past, we do it without even realising it, and to say that you've never been hypocritical, is most probably naive, but you can learn from that feeling. As soon as you show to yourself that you are not a hypocrite, this will radiate to your friends and family. People will start to trust you more because they feel that your opinion is valued and you are a person who truly stands by their word. You become a person that people rely on to help them with their problems because you have their best interest at heart. Helping other people gives a sense of worth and value, and who doesn't love that feeling. You learn who you are, and others get to know the real you because you do not contradict your own beliefs and attitudes and allow others to cloud your judgement and opinions. You do not need to be a hypocrite, you're an amazing person, value your own views, own them, there is nobody else like you, so why would you let anybody affect that?

Chapter Ten: Overcoming Overwhelm

We all feel overwhelmed at some point in our lives. Whether it be uni deadlines creeping up on you and you've left it to the last minute (…again) or your boss breathing down your neck about work reports that needed to be completed 2 weeks ago, and you haven't even started them. But figuring out how to deal with the feeling of overwhelm and not allowing it to fall down a rabbit hole isn't an easy task.

An Amateurs Guide to: Killing It

Take some time

As simple as it sounds, and you've probably heard it 1000 times before. But walking away from a task that is making you feel overwhelmed is the easiest way to not feel overwhelmed. I'm not talking procrastination, but I'm talking about doing something that will ultimately distract your mind. Doing something you love, that reconnects you with happiness. If you're feeling happy, it's challenging to feel overwhelmed at the same time... right? I'm not saying work for 5 minutes, get worked up and then go and party for 4 days. I'm talking about taking ten minutes out of your day to focus yourself and go back to whatever task you need to do with a level head. For me? It's writing. I'm not going to lie to you, I'm writing this chapter right now while I've got 4 uni assignments to write. I was midway through the first one and started feeling overwhelmed, so I've started writing this chapter because writing makes me happy. So find something that makes you happy, and just take your mind off it.

Overtime, you will figure out ways on how to deal with your overwhelming emotion. And I hate to tell you, but this probably will not be the last time you feel overwhelmed. But disconnecting with something temporarily is not always a bad thing, do not feel guilty for allowing yourself to switch off. Happiness is what every person wants to achieve, yes? Focus on the feeling of getting shit done, and it will help you turn from feeling overwhelmed into feeling empowered. Then, you will be unstoppable.

Set Goals

Every Sunday night, I sit down and write down 3 goals for that week. I'll write down a personal goal, a work goal and a learning goal (these will change for you depending on what you have going on in your life at the moment). So, once I have my three goals, I'll then plan time to achieve them. Say for example, as I'm writing this chapter now (it is a Sunday), My learning goal is to write 200 words for my dissertation, my personal goal is to meditate for 10 minutes every day, and my work goal is to finish another chapter of my book. I have then planned time around my day to achieve these goals and actually get things done. This helps with the overwhelming feeling of everything being too much. This is because you can clearly see in front of you what your goals and tasks are for that week. Everybody has a lot of their plate, but the things that aren't vitally important in that week can wait, plan them next Sunday. Start your week with a clear structure of how you want your week to go. Not only will this help you calm down that overwhelming feeling, but it will also allow you to start feeling positive about how your week is going to go before it's even begun. By setting yourself small goals and actually achieving them, you'll feel a lot more productive than if you just complete tasks and do not give yourself the satisfaction of completing them.

Focusing on 'the now' can really improve your overwhelming feeling. Overwhelm is caused by thoughts of the future, the sense of everything building upon you at once. The present moment that you are in right now is the most important. You can't change the future, and right now, you are okay, you are still breathing, people still love you, everything is okay. The future cannot be changed by overwhelming thoughts creeping up on you. Take those thoughts and transform them into energy, to help you project your feelings into passion, and from there, nothing is unachievable, and things will work out, but from this present moment, focus on the now.

Calm your breathing down

It's a lot harder to make rational decisions when your heart is beating at 400 beats per minute. My Dad always says to me, "Don't make commitments when you're happy and don't make decisions when you're sad," and he was so right. Take time to breathe. Focus on your breathing for 2 minutes, and allow yourself to calm down. Then make decisions. Don't go into making decisions when you're overwhelmed. If I did this, I'm pretty sure I would have made the decision to throw my laptop out the window a good few times. Give yourself time to make a decision. Every decision is the right one, at that moment, but make it with a level head rather than making it with the haze of emotions clouding your judgement.

Prioritise

Take a second to prioritise all of the tasks that you have to complete and work strategically. If you've got things that need doing by the next day, obviously, do them first and work your way back to things that aren't as important or can be postponed. I always have a section on my to-do-list called "Back Burner." This is filled with tasks that I know need to be completed, but they have no urgency to be completed within a deadline. This allows you to have a lot more structure to your daily tasks and can take away some of this overwhelming feeling as you realise that everything doesn't need to be completed in that very moment. Sometimes you'll have a to-do-list full of urgent things that need to be completed, and that is okay, just carry on working through your list, take on one task at a time and keep going until it's done. Another thing my Dad has told me about is the analogy of Swiss cheese and task completion. You go into a task and do not stop until it's finished (implying you go in one hole and keep going until you're out the other side), and if your to-do list is full of urgency, it's time to get down and dirty with the cheese. Just remember, your task list will not be urgent forever, even though it may seem that way. Keep battling through it and keep your priorities on lock.

Get up close and personal with the reality of not being perfect

This was difficult for me to write because it took a long time for me to accept this within myself. I have been a perfectionist, for as long as I can remember, and to accept that perfection isn't an attainable goal, really hit hard, but the sooner you realise that 'perfect' doesn't exist, the easier overwhelm is to deal with. Contributions to feeling overwhelm include feeling you have to complete every task without fault, but we all make fuck-ups. It's so much easier to recognise that we all live in an imperfect world than to convince ourselves that our best efforts are never good enough. Being imperfect allows you to move forward and learn from experience, which is what you need when feeling overwhelmed. You need to learn how to improve, and this is only going to be achieved through trial and error. Overwhelming yourself with the idea of something that doesn't exist, is a waste of energy. Perfection doesn't exist. You are doing an amazing job.

Regardless of how prepared you are for the feeling of overwhelm, it's just one of these things that can creep up on you at any time, and that is okay. Do not punish yourself for feeling overwhelmed, it happens to all of us. We all have breakdowns and setbacks, but that is not a sign of failure, that is a lesson that you have grown from and allows you to become a stronger person. It will get better, it always does.

An Amateurs Guide to: Killing It

Chapter Eleven: Changing "What if's" to "whens"

Some people set their alarms last night to wake up this morning, and they never did. Some people made plans last week for this week but didn't make it. There will be people making plans with their families for events in the future that they'll never attend. The only time that you have guaranteed is the present. This is the only time, in this very second, where certainty lies. You are here, in this moment of now and you have no idea what will happen tomorrow, next week, or what might even happen within the next hour. First of all, I apologise for starting this chapter so morbidly; however, I feel it's essential to get the point across. THE ONLY TIME THAT IS CERTAIN IS NOW. So, tell me, why are you constantly putting off your goals and aspirations? "I'll get round to it." "I'll do it tomorrow." Tomorrow isn't guaranteed Stop taking time for granted because none of us truly know when that time will run out, or what will run out, or what will happen that will change the course of our time. Take action now.

'If people do not laugh at your dreams when you tell them, they're not big enough.' The first step of changing your dreams into goals is by writing them down. As soon as you write down a dream, it becomes a goal. From that goal, you create a plan, and from that plan comes an action to go towards it. Working backwards is key. So, take me, for example. I was just writing a blog one day and then had a sudden thought to write a book. The first thing I did was to write it in my annual plan (I'll get to this). Straight away, the thought became a goal. From there, I knew the end product was to have a completed book, so I thought about things like how many chapters I needed to write and how long it would take me to write them. I then set myself mini goals to complete individual sections within specific time frames. This gave me the motivation I needed to complete them (alongside the constant reminder from Ruth to actually get this book finished (I can never thank you enough for that)). Sometimes I wouldn't meet the deadlines I had initially set myself, and I knew that was okay, I just postponed them slightly. Why am I telling you this? This provides one small example of how writing down your dreams can allow for 'what if' to become 'when.' My thought of 'what if I wrote a book,' became a 'when I finish my book' which led to you sitting here with this in your hand right now.

The trick is changing your vocabulary. You need to get used to saying 'when I do that' rather than ' If I do that.' Start using the vocabulary of an achiever. 'If' leads you down a path of uncertainty. Starting your sentence for your future with 'if' shows that you are not confident enough in what you want to do. You end up slowly meandering down your journey, not really having a direction, just aimlessly wandering through a forest of 'if's' hoping something might catch your eye. You're not about that. As soon as you start beginning your future plans with 'when,' your path becomes a lot more definite. You finally have a direction and a drive. You stop aimlessly strolling and start using a vehicle of motivation to get you to your destination.

146

Consciousness is key. To be able to get ahead and to start achieving things in your life, you really need to become aware of the moment of now. YOU NEED TO BE SPECIFIC IN WHAT YOU WANT TO ACHIEVE. Remember way back in chapter one, I said that we'd go into detail on the 1 year, 3-year, and 5-year plan? Yeah, here we are. We made it. So, let me explain this in a bit more detail. To change your "what if" to "when", you need to write down everything that you are aspiring to do, and I mean everything. Write down precisely what you want to achieve, in 1 year, exactly what you want to accomplish in 3 years and exactly what you want to achieve in 10 years and be specific. For example, when I started writing this book, my one year plan was to have 5 recorded songs by the end of the year, finish this book and have my own personal website live (all in which are on track to being achieved, because I set them as personal goals). The more specific you are with your goal writing, the more driven you are going to be in accomplishing them. This is because you gain clarity and consciousness when writing them. You start to visualise yourself in those moments, you feel that success, you become hungry for how you're going to feel when finally achieve that goal. Once you have your goals written out, in exactly what you want to achieve, you then work backwards from them, working out small steps on how to eventually reach that goal. For example, say your goal in 1 year is to lose some weight. Losing *some* weight. You need to be specific and realistic about how much weight you want to lose. Take it one step at a time. Let's say you want to lose 14 pounds. Break it down into 2 pounds a week goals, and then work out your daily calorie intake to lose 2 pounds in weight a week. Then add in maybe a brisk jog around the park every day. Add in things that are relevant to help you achieve your goals and break them down into mini achievements. So, although your goal is to lose a stone in weight, your mini-goal of losing 2 pounds a week sounds a lot less daunting and a lot more achievable than losing a stone straight away. That's just one example of breaking your goals down into small-sized chunks which eventually allow you to realise that you are taking small steps towards success.

I will get onto this a little later, however acknowledging that you have come so far, is vital in changing your vocabulary. Constant and never-ending improvement is so unbelievably important. Society today puts so much pressure on people to feel like they can continually achieve more, and that they continuously need to work harder. What we miss out on is what we have already achieved. You have achieved so much, and you are so much stronger than you think. People are always striving for more, and feel like they fail when they can't achieve that. It becomes so easy to forget what you have already done because you replace it with the feeling of wanting something more, something bigger and something more rewarding. But you forget the drive that it took you to get to the point you are already at.

You need to appreciate the small victories that you achieve. We have ingrained the idea that nothing is good enough, you close one item on your to-do list and open 6 more, right? I'm not telling you to reward yourself with a trip to the Bahama's every week because you've managed to submit your stat report on time (even though you should DEFINITELY do this). I'm telling you to give yourself a round of applause. Sounds stupid right? "What will people think of me if I just start randomly clapping in the street because I've just secured that client" FUCK THAT. Give yourself a clap. A fucking round of applause. You smashed it. By doing that small token of appreciation to yourself, you're going to feel like you are achieving something rather than constantly not feeling like you're doing enough. Through this, you're drawing more conscious attention to the fact that you have achieved something, rather than just constantly replacing it with the strive for more. Don't get me wrong, it's incredible that you're pushing yourself to be the best you can be, and I'm not saying stop that. All I'm saying is give yourself a clap because you're fucking amazing.

So, now what. Now you go and grab a pen, and you write down what you actually want to achieve in the next year, 3 years and 5 years, and you work back from that. Sure, you might not do this right now, don't get me wrong, I read A LOT of self-help books that were telling me to do this before I actually decided to do it. But, from experience, let me tell you, the moment that I wrote my dreams and aspirations down and turned them into goals, was the moment that motivation and drive hit me like a tonne of bricks and since then I have been unstoppable. What is stopping you, why wait? Time is going to continue, whether you decide to take action now, or you wait until later. But don't let 10 years go past, and then realise "Shit, I probably should have done something in those 10 years". Take action now, and MAKE THOSE PLANS.

Chapter Twelve: Decision Making

We all have those times in our lives where we have to make life-altering decisions. Well, what seems life-altering. This can be scary, I get that, sometimes your first instinct is to shy away from making those decisions because it's easier than having to face them. Face what could be consequences from them. Face the fact you might have to make sacrifices. But hey, change is a good thing, change makes things interesting, it's scary but so worth it. Sometimes, you might make the bad decisions, but that's okay, we all make mistakes, but it's how you deal with the consequences from that decision that allows you to focus the next decision you have to make. I'm writing this chapter because I am currently facing some big decisions that I'm going to have to make in my life. I was talking to my friend the other day about what I need to do about these decisions, and that I was feeling very on edge about making them because of the effect that they might have. "What if I make the wrong decision", isn't that what goes through everyone's mind when they have to make choices?

Every decision that you make is the right decision. It's your life, so whatever your decision you make, good or bad, it's never wrong. Sure we can all make bad decisions, but you learn from them. Learning from the choices you have previously made is so important, it helps you to become a better and stronger person. Stop punishing yourself for the decisions that you make that might seem like bad decisions at the time. As long as your happiness is the first priority, any decision you make is the right one. Sometimes your choices may change your life path, for example, a new job, deciding to go travelling or enter a relationship with someone new. Big decisions are tough to make. But do not shy away from decision making because you're scared of what might come. Get excited about where it might lead you. Transform fear into positive energy. "I am making these decisions to better my life and make myself happy." This should be your priority in every decision you make.

Another thing that makes decision making even harder is the people around you that it may affect. This is when you need to make a choice on top of your decision. How is it going to affect the people around you and will it affect your happiness if you restrict yourself to save the feeling of others. This is your life, and the people who are meant to be in, it will stay by your side through every decision that you decide to make, no matter how life-altering that may be. With FaceTime, and every social media platform allowing you to message people on the other side of the world, staying in contact has never been so easy. The people who mean the most to you will remain in your life. Distance is merely a number. So if your decision means moving away or travelling, but you're scared about leaving everybody behind, you're not. It's so easy to bring people along on the journey with you. So do something for yourself, take that step to make your life better for yourself. People will stay on the journey with you, and if they decide not to, leave it at that, be grateful for the memories they gave you, and move on to make more.

Decisions can make you feel overwhelmed, especially if you have many of them to make in a small amount of time. This is where pro and con lists come into play. Remember in Friends when Ross made that list about Rachel and Julie to help him choose which one to date? Like that. But minus the drama. Take the time to write down everything that you need to make decisions for and make lists. Write down everything good about that decision and everything not so good. Then once you're at the end of your list, it will become apparent which choice you need to make. If the pros outweigh the cons, then it's obvious you need to take the plunge and do something for you.

Stop being afraid of worrying what could come from your decisions, and start envisioning how much better your life could be if you take these opportunities. You are in the driver seat for your decision making, realistically when you're twenty years older, are you going to regret not travelling the world because you were scared? No. Do not replace fear with regret.

Give yourself as much time as possible

Hasty decisions often end in negative outcomes. Think about the consequences of your choices. I'm all for spontaneity, however, sometimes you need the time to think about your decisions and the impact that they can have. For example, I'm all for you upping and leaving your job to go and travel the world, as long as you've thought about how you're going to be making an income, or if you even need one. Go and make the spontaneous decisions, but make sure that you have back up plans, so that if things do not go according to plan, you've got an exit route, whether that be extra money in your savings, or getting long term leave from work, always give yourself enough time to make safety nets for your spontaneous decisions.

An Amateurs Guide to: Killing It

Know when to let go of a lost cause

With making difficult decisions, you might restrict yourself from making choices that will benefit your future because you're putting all your energy into something that just isn't worth it. Going back to my Dad, we were having dinner one day, and he was telling me about this analogy about a boat. He says to me, "Shannon if you have to struggle upstream, it's not meant to be, put your oars into your boat and just go downstream." He was so right. Stop fighting for decisions that just aren't meant to be, this just wastes both your time and energy. The journey is a lot easier when you stop struggling to reach decisions that do not need to be made. This links back to the idea that every decision is a right one, and hey, your boat might hit a couple rocks on the way down, might even capsize, but you will always have the strength to repair it because you've stopped paddling upstream. If you don't make the decisions, the decisions will make you. People still deem this as a massive negative thing, but is it? Is it a problem that

you let the decisions that life throws at you define you? No.

Life will make decisions for you, it's how you deal with those

decisions that matter.

Chapter Thirteen: Discovering Self Confidence

"Just believe in yourself" if only it were this easy, right? Whether it be sweaty palms before a class presentation or trying to rationalise your racing thoughts, we all go through times of doubting ourselves, and this can have long-lasting effects. Here are a few tips on how to deal with rebuilding broken self-confidence.

Prepare to deliver

A massive part of self-confidence is the fear of failure, therefore, planning ahead prevents the thought of failure even entering your mind. Prepare for that presentation by rehearsing it, plan your day so that it goes precisely how you want it to. This takes practice. You're not going to be able to start planning perfectly from the get-go, and that is okay. Stick with it, allow yourself plenty of time before deadlines to get things done (I know first hand this is difficult, and life gets in the way, however, be conscious of the time you have before tasks are due instead of continually pushing things back). The more time you allow yourself to prepare for things, the more confident you're going to become because you have the time to produce your best work. You'll find you have more faith in yourself that you're going to ace it because you have had time to adequately prepare yourself and therefore your self-confidence towards delivering that task will increase.

Be present

Fear is an emotion that is a big part of self-confidence. You are only ever afraid of things that haven't happened yet. Take falling, for example. Nobody wants to fall from a great height.

However, once you're falling, you're no longer afraid of falling, you're scared of hitting the ground. So, if you are present in the moment, it's pretty difficult to be scared of failure. Take every day at a time, acknowledge, and live in every moment. Immerse yourself in the present instead of fearing the future. If you're present, your decisions will seem a lot more relaxed, and you'll feel more confident in those decisions because they are made out of instinct, not fear. You'll adapt the "things are meant to happen this way" mindset, and confidence comes with that, you are doing the right thing, this is your journey, own it.

Learn who you are

To be fully self-confident, you need to get to know yourself. You wouldn't be confident in a strangers decision that they make for you, so why would you treat yourself as a stranger.

Get to know yourself, go out and face your fears, find your limits and push them, I'm telling you to go out and make mistakes because although this is a difficult thought, there is no such thing as failure, just feedback. You will learn from your mistakes, and become more confident in the decisions that you do end up making because of the setbacks you've had in the past. To walk forward, you've got to project from your past. Think of it like walking, you push off with your back foot, right? Think of this as your setbacks, use them to push you forward, the further you want to go, the harder you've got to push off that back foot. Failure is feedback, and feedback grows your self-confidence because it allows you to branch out your thoughts and move forward. Keep moving forward, you're doing an amazing job. Keep going.

Let's talk a moment about something that affects us all so much. Social media. How many times have you uploaded to social media and checked your phone 40 times within the first hour to make sure you haven't missed one notification on your new selfie or the new photo you've uploaded of your dog walk? You've become imprisoned by your phone, and for the next day and a half you end up basing your mood and self-esteem on the number of likes you've received. If your post performs better than you think, oxytocin (the love hormone) floods into your veins as you feel overjoyed with the amount of love you've been shown from your loyal following. You feel appreciated, and you feel like this moment was 'worth' sharing. But let's address what happens when your post doesn't get as many likes as you had initially anticipated.

Don't get me wrong, you might be one of these people who aren't affected by social media likes, and I take my hat off to you, I really do. However, if you are one of those individuals who know you base your mood on 'likes,' keep reading. So, let's say your latest photo didn't get as many likes as you thought. You tell yourself that you must have posted at the wrong time, and your followers haven't seen your post. You become angry at them for not liking your post. Might even message them and direct them to your post. You then might fall into self-doubt. End up telling yourself that your photo just wasn't good enough, maybe you didn't show enough skin, perhaps too much. You paint these assumptions in your head with a permanent marker and make yourself feel unworthy of posting what you did. So, what do people do now? They might completely delete their post and try again later. They might buy likes to increase the popularity of their post to make them feel more appreciated, or potentially delete the memory from their feed forever. Tell me this, why has it become that we judge our value based on a virtual thing? How has social media dictated whether you feel worthy? Whether you feel pretty enough is based on an algorithm of how many people see your post at that time? Social media is addictive, and this is becoming an ongoing problem for people with low self-esteem who are relying on virtual things to soothe their insecurities. This is an issue that is so easily overlooked because most people are in the same boat. We all use social media, probably a lot more than we should. We've all sat down on the sofa after a long say of telling yourself that you are going to have a productive evening to then scroll through hours of Facebook and Instagram videos without realising where the time went. Daily we are overlooking the meaning behind what we post on our social media because of the fear of what other people think or if they will leave us a 'like.' We forget our value, our self worth is replaced with the addiction of approval and social acceptance. Just take one moment to realise the things that meant so much more to you than that one like on social media.

1. The people you shared that memory with. Acknowledge the fact that your Instagram post had a

purpose. Whether it was a night out on the town with your best friends or the cake, you made with your Nan last week. The post has a lot more meaning than the photo at face value. Appreciate the memory that comes with it.

2. Go and find the people that you've shut off because you're pissed off about them not liking your photo and go and create more memories with them. Go for lunch, give them a call, stop restricting future memories because you've closed your mind based on an online heart-shaped button.

3. Appreciate the fact you had the confidence to post in the first place. Posting when you have one thousand plus followers as an audience can be daunting, but be proud of the fact that you had the courage to post it. Go you!

An Amateurs Guide to: Killing It

We need to work together on this. Social media addiction is overlooked so quickly, and we need to bring it to light. So, instead of putting that girl down because she posted a photo you deemed 'slutty,' think twice. Our issue as a society is we shoot people down too fast, and people destroy people's confidence that takes years to build. By bitching about people's posts behind their back, you end up just adding fuel to the fire. Whether they want to post 150 selfies a day, or they want to fill it with pictures of their favourite aeroplanes, regardless of your opinion, it's their profile, and they have the right to do so. Instead of continually trying to make your profile what you think others might want to see, make it your own. With that, you'll become more understanding of people's posts, and help to eliminate the idea that social media likes dictate your self worth and confidence because you have so much more worth than a number on a post.

Self-confidence is something that will only come with time. You are the most important person to you. Appreciate who you are as a person and treat yourself with the upmost respect because you deserve no less.

Chapter Fourteen: Demolishing boundaries and extending horizons

We all set ourselves boundaries. Sometimes without even realising that you've set them, they just appear. Have you ever tried to do something entirely out of the blue and then had the feeling of not being able to do it? Even though you've never experienced what it feels like before? Welcome to the art of subconscious boundary setting, not going to lie to you, this one can be a bit of a bitch to master, but we'll do it together. We set ourselves boundaries for different reasons, and the first way to extend them is by analysing why they were established in the first place.

One reason that your mind sets you boundaries is to protect yourself, think of it as a safety net if you like. Something to fall back on if you fail. If you have limits, it's gonna stop you from doing things that you are unsure about. For example, your boundary might be the thought that you will never be able to jump out of a plane because you have a crippling fear of heights. Therefore, your boundary is set because your mind knows that jumping from a plane can be a high-risk activity, and being high up can cause you the risk of being hurt. The boundary becomes solidly set in your mind that you will never be able to experience a parachute jump because your mind is trying to protect you (just for the record, parachute jumping was one of the best things that I've ever done, and I'd recommend it to anybody in a heartbeat).

Your mental boundaries also come up for self-doubt. The feeling that you might not be able to achieve something. Barriers like these tend to arise around things like going to University even though you're forty or learning a new language that you've never learned before. These boundaries are ones that we all have because you might be scared to fail. Scared people will laugh at us. We set the belief that we will not succeed. If your boundary says that you do not have the capability of learning a new language of getting that degree, then you eliminate the possibility of failure because you never try.

Fear. This is a MASSIVE boundary that so many of us share. Fear of failure, a fear of being wrong, a fear of making the wrong decision. We all have fears. This boundary is strongly linked with protection because fear does nothing but try to protect you. However, the amount of opportunities that you are missing out on because of this bullshit thing called fear is insane.

An Amateurs Guide to: Killing It

"Everything you have ever wanted is on the other side of Fear" - George

Addir

I introduce you to my favourite quote of all time, and one that has definitely changed my outlook on this whole "fear" thing. Fear is just an emotion, just like happiness and sadness. Nothing more. Fear does not dictate your life. You are more than your fears. They do not define you, only you define you. Something that really hit home with me when talking about fear is the idea that is always in the future. You can never fear something that is in the present. How can you be afraid of something that hasn't happened yet?

Take time to focus your energy on yourself and extending your own personal horizons. Sometimes, all you need is a few seconds of extreme courage to try to extend that mental barrier for you to achieve something amazing. The hardest part about extending your personal boundaries is the idea that it might be a very lonely journey. It's not until you try to put past what once was mentally blocking you, that you truly understand what and who was holding you back. Some people pass through your life for a reason, and they teach you lessons that you never truly would have understood if they stayed. Be grateful for the fact that you can continuously move forward and do not be afraid of leaving people behind. The people around you who genuinely care about you and want you to grow and be the best you can be will grow with you. To extend that barrier you need to stop chasing after other people and constantly try to fix everything for everybody else (I struggle with this too, it's hard, I'll be the first to admit it). It's physically and mentally draining. To fully be able to push yourself further than even you thought you could go, you need to find inner peace within yourself and learn that the only things you truly need to 'fix' are things that affect you and your life. Don't be the only one putting in the effort, just to lose yourself for trying to save everybody else because your mental barrier will stay very close.

You might think that you have pushed yourself further than you ever have before and that you can't push yourself anymore. That's amazing. To feel you've pushed yourself and achieved something is an amazing feeling. But the vital thing to remember here, is you need to learn how to rest and not quit. Reward yourself for pushing yourself, take some time to rejuvenate yourself and your goals, and then push on, push harder. Everything begins to change when you love yourself. Your energy is sourced from positivity and peacefulness rather than being created through anger and frustration. As soon as that switch flicks, you will learn who you are and learn that you do not need the constant approval of other people. You are truly unstoppable, there is nobody else like you. You can push harder, you can do this. Short term pain. Long term gain.

Chapter Fifteen: Acknowledging Success

"You're so lucky." People's first judgment when you start succeeding. You got your promotion because you got lucky. You finally got that job that you've always wanted because you got lucky. People miss out on the hours of work you put in behind the scenes. The sleepless nights, the tears, the hard work. The constant networking and constant reach out of your comfort zone. It's not luck. It's hard work. The people who will tell you that "you're just lucky" are afraid to push themselves. By putting success down to luck, they have a "valid" excuse to wait for success to come to them. That is not how it works. You want success? You get up earlier than your competition. You work harder than you ever have. You push yourself to your mental and physical limits. Every. Single. Day. No excuses. Your success is a reflection of your hard work, do not be ashamed of that. Be proud of it.

Success doesn't have to be earning millions of pounds a year. Success can be something as small as you finally started that blogging channel you've been putting off, starting that YouTube channel that you've been scared to for so long or starting your own business. Success comes on so many levels, but it takes work to climb up that ladder. Sometimes you get boosts and perks which will make your climb more straightforward, but you chose the mountain to climb, that wasn't luck. Getting to the top, that isn't luck, it's a combination of commitment, consistency, and motivation. Life isn't about the destination, it's the journey that matters.

Get yourself an achievement journal to keep track of everything you achieve. Whether that be finishing that big essay you've had for months or something as small as remembering to take all of your medication. By acknowledging the fact that you are continually making progress, you will appreciate every personal "win" you make. In the words of Benjamin Franklin, "Without continual growth and progress, such words as improvement, achievement, and success have no meaning." To truly appreciate the fact that you have improved, you need to acknowledge the fact that you are progressing, slowly, but continuously. With an achievement journal, it also provides subconscious encouragement to strive to do more. You will find yourself finding things that you can write in there to add to the journey. You set yourself smaller goals just so you can write them in your journal because it feels good to achieve something. Then, when you have feelings of doubt or the feeling that you might not be able to accomplish a task, you can look back at all you have achieved and almost self-coach yourself into realising your potential as an individual. You have achieved so much already, you can achieve more. You have 100% got this.

Reward yourself. Whether that be with nap time (my personal favourite kind of reward) or going out for drinks with your friends on the weekend after you meet a deadline. Find little things that you can reward yourself with to give yourself a sense of achievement. This will also help you to encourage and motivate yourself to get shit done and stop postponing it. The earlier you get the task started and completed, the earlier you get the reward. You deserve it. Life isn't like the high jump. Let me explain where I'm going with this. You set the bar high, and you manage to get over it. But instead of raising the bar straight away to the next level, reward yourself for jumping at that height. People too often think that because they jumped at that height and cleared it, the task was too easy, the jump wasn't advanced enough. This isn't the case. You still had to set your mind to the jump, regardless of the height, you cleared the bar. We always strive for a new personal best, however, learn to acknowledge the fact that you cleared the previous jump, and you can clear the next one.

Look, the fact that you've made it to this chapter is a success in itself. Be proud of yourself for finishing something you set out to do. By picking this book up, you already showed yourself that you wanted to change your outlook on your life, and the fact that you've made it this far shows that you have the commitment and willpower to finish what you start. This is the first step for you becoming the best "you" you can be. This is a personal achievement. The start of the new you. You no longer need approval from everybody else. You are your own person, you are proud of that, and you are stronger than ever. You can achieve anything that you set your mind to, and you are genuinely fucking KILLING IT.

So, now what? Do you close this book, never to re-read it, let it collect dust on your shelf (or memory on whatever device you are reading this on)? Forget everything I've spent hundreds of hours to write down to help you improve your life? Who knows? That decision is down to you and only you. If you chose to re-read specific chapters as you experience tough times, then go for it. If you read this and you don't think it's the right time for you to action what you've learned from this book, then that's okay too. This is your journey, and it's been a real honour to be apart of it. I want to personally thank you for allowing me the opportunity embark on this journey with you. If there is anything you take away from this book, the one thing it would be is, please remember, no decision is the wrong decision, because this is your life. You have totally got this. You are killing it, be proud of yourself because I couldn't be prouder of you. I look forward to hearing about your success stories. Let's do this.

An Amateurs Guide to: Killing It

A lasting note

First of all, thank you. I can't thank you enough for supporting me through reading this. The support that I've received through writing my first book is honestly overwhelming, and it's thanks to individuals like yourself who have given this a chance. The journey that I have been on through the last year while writing this has probably been the toughest yet most rewarding year of my life. I can't thank my friends, family, and supporters enough for consistently being there when I need them. Thank you for believing in me. We all have this power within us to do amazing things, and there is no time like the present. I don't know who needs to hear this right now, but JUST FUCKING DO IT. We're all amateurs in our own journey, but you are still here, you're consistently improving, and you're killing it.

An Amateurs Guide to: Killing It

Helplines:

Samaritans 24 hours a day, 365 days a year. You can call 116 123 (free from any phone)

 SANEline on 0300 304 7000 (4.30pm–10.30pm every day)

If you're under 25, you can call The Mix on 0808 808 4994 (Sunday-Friday 2pm–11pm)

If you're under 35 and struggling with suicidal feelings, or concerned about a young person who might be struggling, you can call Papyrus HOPELINEUK on 0800 068 4141 (weekdays 10am-10pm, weekends 2pm-10pm and bank holidays 2pm–10pm)

An Amateurs Guide to: Killing It

"Everything you have ever wanted, is on the other side of

fear" - George Addir.

An Amateurs Guide to: Killing It

An Amateurs Guide to: Killing It

An Amateurs Guide to: Killing It

An Amateurs Guide to: Killing It

A Special thanks to Ruth and Sarah for consistently asking me when this book was going to be finished, and for pushing me to actually finish something I set out to do.

Printed in Great Britain
by Amazon

85662796R00112